Angel Power and How to Use It

Angel Power and How to Use It

by

Reverend Polette Carabel

DORRANCE PUBLISHING CO., INC.
PITTSBURGH, PENNSYLVANIA 15222

ISBN # 0-8059-3957-1
Printed in the United States of America

First Printing

For information or to order additional books, please write:
Dorrance Publishing Co., Inc.
643 Smithfield Street
Pittsburgh, Pennsylvania 15222-2505
U.S.A.

A TRIBUTE

Here's to an Angel leaving
her healing mark upon this
Earth. Pollete Parabel's
hands soothed and healed
my understanding (my feet)
and my life beat (my soul.)
with the strength and gentleness
only an Angel can manage.

Betsy Palmer
Actress

Betsy Palmer

A Testament

I have been married to Poleete for many years now, although it seems like a very short time. Her Angel class was my real discovery of what and who she is, which was twenty-five years ago—and she has taught an Angel class every year since then, and I attended them all.

When she relates some of the healings she was a part of, you can multiply that number by hundreds. She has been a healer since she was a little child and became a dedicated participant with the power of God and His Angels in all the healings.

This book is a partial record of a person who lives her life as Jesus taught and demonstrated. Poleete loves everyone. We know that God is love and it is the love of which Jesus spoke and that made possible His healings and the manifestations we call miracles. She has been an inspiration to me from our first meeting, and is still an inspiration today.

Whether you are a student of the truth or not, you will find this book understandable, interesting and inspirational. Angel Power is all around you, just waiting for your call.

Ben

Angel Power and How to Use It reaches into the depths of every person's problems and solves them by using these purely spiritual techniques: simplified and yet profound. We are entering the age of the Angels, which places us in an entirely new world where only Harmony, Joy, and Love reign. *Angel Power and How to Use It* was Divinely inspired and I was the instrument through which it came.

"Prayer is the door to the Kingdom of God
and Faith is the key that unlocks it."

Contents

Preface

Everyone is acquainted with computers and their miraculous workings. But as miraculous as they are, tuning the Angels in is a hundred times more so. Almost every day the inventors are improving computers. You can learn every day how to improve your contact with the Angel World. It is immense and endless. And just as you have to learn by diligence and discipline how to use a computer, you have to learn how to use the glorious fulfilling Love of the Angels the same way.

First you have to believe and have faith. You couldn't learn to use a computer unless you believed you could and had faith in yourself. The same is true with the Angels, except that you must approach this study from a purely spiritual standpoint where the computer is a material object that you can see, feel, and touch. The Angels can be felt and many, many people have seen them. I can honestly say that they have never failed me because I believe so sincerely.

God created the Angels for a specific purpose—to "have charge over us all in all our ways." The 91st Psalm tells you this in no uncertain words. There are over 240 references to Angels in the Bible. They played very extensive roles in the lives of many great people whose lives attested to their powerful contact, such as Mary, the mother of Jesus. It was the Angel Gabriel that told her she was to bear the Christ child; Angels protected Daniel in the lion's den and kept the furious animals from devouring him; Angels broke the chains from John's wrists, put the guards to sleep and allowed John to escape from his unjust imprisonment. When Moses was leading the children of Israel out of bondage, the Angels appeared as fire by night and clouds by day to show Moses where to go and to protect the people who had been so long enslaved by the Egyptians. These are just a few of the instances of the appearance of Angels and their mighty mission in aiding mankind.

Everyone can have the Power of Angels in his or her life if they want it enough to earn it. How? By building a bridge of qualities from this so-called human existence into the Angel World. Each plank, made of gold, that we build, has written upon it the words that take us into this Divine Heritage, if we live them and abide in them. The first plank in your bridge is blazoned with the word *love*. You have to feel a great love, not only for the Angels, but for all mankind. As you erect your bridge you build it with great joy because that is one of the largest planks in your bridge. Then when you complete it with beautiful words you can expect the Angels to use it and to come to you. They are always ready with open arms to receive you, but you have to make the effort by preparing your consciousness on the highest level possible.

As you make your bridge, place your jewels of good deeds and good thoughts on the side of each plank. Then it will be a thing of beauty and give the precious Angels an easy access to you in every walk of your life. If you do this daily you will find that you are "entertaining" Angels as constant guests and great friends. Angels are not imaginary beings, they are as real as you are. They are "God's Representatives."

Chapter One
Healings and Revealings

When I wrote my first book, *Poleete,* I did so hesitatingly—this one I do with joy. I've had so many wonderful experiences that my story begged to be written.

Before I begin, I must tell you of the marvelous happening that occurred with my book *Poleete.* While I was writing it the Angels bid me write it very simply—using simple language. I did so. At the time I was teaching an Angel class and attending my class was a young woman named Jackie who worked as a secretary for the president of a large company. This man had a son, Roger, who had a brain tumor operation a year before and the tumor seemed to have returned, leaving Roger paralyzed on one side of his body and with a bad speech defect as well. The doctors told his parents that his case was hopeless and that he had no chance of survival and could die at any moment. Jackie knew the mother, and of course was acquainted with the seventeen-year-old Roger. She asked his parents if Roger could visit her for a while, and they consented. Jackie then called me; she knew I was in the healing work, and told me all about Roger and asked for my help, which I gladly gave. Jackie had purchased my book, and while she was at work the next day, Roger read it. When she returned, this was the conversation that ensued.

"Jackie, I just finished your book by Poleete Carabel and I understood every word. Your other books on metaphysics were always over my head. This woman could heal me," said Roger.

1

Roger did not know that Jackie had already called me. "Okay, Roger," replied Jackie. "I'll take off work tomorrow and ask Poleete if we can see her."

I cleared my day and of course I was available for this young man. Our first meeting was very successful. I spiritualized Roger's name and I taught him not to fear the future because now is the only time, and that the next day at the same hour it would still be now, and while we were together at that moment we were entering a new world—a new state of consciousness. Roger grasped things very quickly and his healing started at once. Roger then attended my Bible class and the entire group witnessed his remarkable healing. He went from being a dying young boy to a very handsome and healthy young man. He again attended college and today is married and living a normal life. All because I listened to the Angels!

Before I go any further in my book, I want to share with all my readers a magical formula that I received from the Angels some time ago. I've shared this with all the people in my classes and every one of them has had very marvelous results. Here it is. If you are facing a problem with a person, for instance, take the name of the particular party and put a spiritualization by each letter of his or her name. If it is a company or a corporation, use the name of that company. If it is a court case, use the names of everyone concerned. I will detail some of the results which I have personally witnessed.

One day my husband introduced me to a young man who asked him to invest in a restaurant with him. My husband wanted my approval in the deal. I talked to the young man, whose name was Sam, and I frankly told him that I knew he was a fraud. He was handsome, beautifully groomed, highly educated, and came from a family of means. He laughed at me when I said, "Sam, I see you behind bars." I had never met him before, and I knew nothing about any of his business deals, but intuitively I saw that he was a very clever con man. He tried to talk me into the proposition, but I stood pat, and of course my husband (although he seemed astonished) backed me up. Sam then asked me to teach him metaphysics. For the first and last time so far, I refused to teach him by saying, "Sam, it would take me too long to teach you and besides you won't be free."

His rejoinder was, "Want to bet? I'll learn everything you know in three months."

At that point, I felt compassion for this conceited young man, so I said, "Tell you what, Sam, I'll spiritualize your name and give you some Bible references." Samuel's name spiritualized is Safe and he is secure—if he stays under the guidance of Angels and is using the One Mind—God—to Unite him Eternally with the great Love that God, the Masters and Angels have for him. The Light of God *never* fails. Bible passages were from Psalms 91st, 23rd, and I Corinthians Chapter 13.

This pleased him. He took the paper on which I had written his full name, folded it and placed it in his shirt pocket. Two months later he was sent to prison for seven years on several counts of fraud and embezzlement. We heard nothing from Sam or about him for at least four years. One day my husband was walking down a street in Los Angeles and a man approached him, saying, "Ben, you are just the person I wanted to see—and I must see Poleete."

They shook hands, and Ben realized it was Sam—a new Sam, as Ben described to me. A few days later Sam was sitting in our living room, relating this amazing story.

"Poleete, to the last breath in my body, I will never forget what you did for me to change my entire life. I'm sure you didn't realize when you gave me that spiritualization of my name that it would cause such a complete metamorphosis as I have experienced."

"Yes," I replied, "I've seen people change before with this system."

"But never, I'll wager, to the degree that I did," answered Sam.

"You do look entirely different," said Ben, gazing at Sam with astonishment.

"I am—I've changed completely—and of course, for the better. But let me tell you the details; that is, the astounding part. The first day in prison, according to procedure I was sent to the office of the state psychiatrist. I stood in front of his desk and taking the paper you wrote out of my pocket, I laid it on the desk in front of him. He read it with a puzzled expression on his face.

"'Do you believe all of this about yourself?' he asked. I answered in the affirmative. 'Well then, son, you don't need me—but I would like to keep that paper,' he replied.

"I smiled at him and said, 'No way! I will never part with it,' and, Poleete, I never have.

"A few weeks later a young man came into the prison with some metaphysical literature and I asked him to please leave me some of the magazines, as I was interested. I saw that these books were the same ones I had seen in your home. My entire life took a complete turn. I became a Bible student along with Metaphysics, found myself actually doing healing work for the other inmates, and also brought dozens of them into the kind of thinking that I was doing. Time raced by, and one day I was called before the parole board and told that I was being released. Those years that I spent in so-called confinement were the best in my life, and as soon as I have my two children raised, I intend to devote my life to helping the less fortunate and giving them the lessons I have learned, Poleete—all because you loved humanity enough to spiritualize my name. It had to take great love at that time."

I had tears in my eyes when Sam finished his disclosure, and I was extremely grateful to God and his Beloved Angels. Sam has a good position now and is a steady church goer. There have been dozens and dozens of experiences in my life where this system has produced marvelous results—many times beyond expectation—but I will only tell of one that I feel is very important because of the nature of the case.

One of my dear friends and students called me one day saying. "Poleete, I am panicky. I just left the doctor's office where I had to take an examination for my insurance, and he told me that my heart was in such a serious condition that he could not give me the O.K. I needed for the insurance company. What shall I do?"

"Just calm down," I said, "and come over. Call your doctor and tell him you will return for another examination in two weeks."

My friend came, and we spiritualized not only her name, but the word "heart." Two weeks later she went into a hospital for just the day, to have a thorough examination. She said she was saying her Angel prayers out loud during the entire session. She came through it with flying colors and a perfect record. You see, her "faith made her whole," and she remains that way.

This healing occurred in my own family to my niece. I told of this healing in my first book, but am recounting it again, this time giving the procedure I used.

Allana was nine years of age when she came to me and asked for a healing. It seems that the child had been born with crippled feet. She had never been able to dance or even run with the other children. She walked on the sides of her feet with one foot turned inward. Her mother finally took her to a foot doctor, who X-rayed her feet and said the problem was in the fact that she had too many bones in each foot. He told her she would have to undergo an operation with both feet placed in a cast for several weeks. That was when Allana came to me. She did not want to face an operation. I took it up at once using the following procedure. First, I looked up the word "bones" in the thesaurus and the dictionary and the meaning behind the word, which stood for "foundation." Then I looked up the word "foot" and found that stood for "understanding." I also looked up the references to feet in my Bible concordance and I came across many marvelous meanings. Then I stayed with the word "form," realizing that God created all form, therefore it had to express absolute perfection. I read this beautiful hymn to Allana, which says in part, "Eternal Mind the potter is, thought the Eternal Clay, the Hand that fashions is Divine, His works pass not way." She listened eagerly and expectantly, so of course she was healed. In two weeks she was running and dancing, and is still doing so with *great gratitude* to God, the Angels, and the Masters. She is grown now, but she still follows the Christ-like Pathway. God Bless her!

This next healing I feel compelled to share because of the nature of the case, and the ramifications surrounding it. I was soloist with a singing group at the time, and we were preparing for an important concert. Living a few blocks from me was a member of the chorus, Maria. She invited me to visit her one day after a rehearsal saying that there was a young man visiting her family from the East who was a pianist, and whom she said wanted to hear me sing, as she had told him about me. I am not (and never have been) a person who just went visiting for no particular purpose. My life has always been too busy for that, but this time I felt a compulsion to accept Maria's invitation, so I went. While she and I were talking about the coming engagement, in walked a young boy of seventeen on crutches. He was introduced to me as Jimmie. Maria asked me if I would sing for him, which I consented to do. He played the piano beautifully for such a young person. My heart went out to him. Maria followed me out to my car. I asked her about Jimmie, and she told me that he had been a victim of polio when he was nine. One leg had never grown, and under his clothing he wore a brace from his shoulders to his waist.

"Poleete," said Maria, "I've heard that you do healing. Could you heal Jimmie? I'll bring him over."

Then, of course, I knew why I had been led to visit her. "All right, Maria," I answered, "bring him Saturday and we will get his Angels busy."

Jimmie came, and I had him spend the day with me. He played the piano, and we talked about his healing and about his beliefs. He had been raised in the Lutheran church, but was amenable to other concepts. He *was*, of course eager to be healed. His mother had passed away when he was very young, and his father had married again. He had a half–brother who seemed to receive all the attention in the family. Jimmie felt left out, and because of his condition he had become a loner, and had buried himself in his music (in which he was very talented). Maria's family had been acquainted with his mother, and had kept in contact with Jimmie. They encouraged his father to let him visit them for a while, so here he was. The Bible states that God has strange ways of showing us his love and this was one of them. The entire incident was certainly not an accidental happening, that I should come into Jimmie's life in a rather strange way.

I had him come over every Saturday. He attended church with me. Soon his crutches were laid aside, and replaced with a cane. Maria's mother had entered him in a school for handicapped children, which he disliked. So after a few weeks, I talked it over with Jimmie and I entered him into a regular high school. I visited all of his teachers, and explained that he might be tardy in some of the classes because he had to go up some steep stairs. They were very cooperative with us, and Jimmie was happy. One night after a couple of weeks, Jimmie called me (it was around midnight) saying, "Poleete, something strange is happening to my leg, it doesn't ache, but it feels tingly."

I thought for a moment and then I said, "Jimmie, your leg is growing—be grateful!"

And sure enough, that was exactly what was happening. The leg outgrew the brace, and he never used it again. We kept up the studying together. Soon Jimmie was playing the organ in Sunday school. He was becoming a very handsome young man. Then one day my friends invited us to a concert, and I knew Jimmie would enjoy that, so I asked if he could attend. These friends picked us up, and I sat in the back seat with Jimmie.

I always gave him affection, because I knew that he needed love. This particular evening, as I put my arms around his shoulders, much to my joy and astonishment, he was not wearing his back braces. He smiled a broad smile and said, "I wanted you to find out for yourself, Poleete. This morning when I went to put my brace on, it broke in three parts—then I knew I didn't need it ever again."

We both wept—not with sadness, but with joy. Jimmie's progress became very fast, and dozens of people witnessed this marvelous healing. His father finally sent for him, and the last letter I received was from college. Jimmie had just finished a concert on the stage at the university, and was riding a new racing bicycle back and forth to classes. These are the events in my wonderful life that make everything so worthwhile. My son, who was a young teenager at the time that Jimmie was in our experiences, states that he would never forget this particular case, in spite of all he has seen and had seen prior to this healing.

I believe this is the time and place to relate an experience that had to do with money. And since money seems to be so uppermost in everyone's thinking, this may help someone to see that money is not such a difficult thing to acquire. The Bible states that "the love of money is the root of all evil." This has to be understood properly. To begin with, money is a high form of substance, but it must be properly understood. When the Bible speaks of it being evil, it does not mean the actual dollar bill, it means the consciousness behind it. If you fear the lack of it that brings evil results (evil meaning a lack of good), if you hoard it, that is evil; if you are greedy, that is evil; if you put it before God, you are breaking the First Commandment, "Thou shall have no other Gods before me." And if you break one Commandment, you have broken them all, because a chain is just as strong as its weakest link. The Ten Commandments are the basis for Christianity, and in fact all religions. If they are broken then one has to pay a Karmic debt. We will go into the subject of Karma later on. Now I want to tell you about this case.

A young man living in another state called me one morning in absolute desperation. His conversation went like this:

"Poleete, I am facing a dreadful situation. My home and my business are going down the drain and I am at my wit's end."

"No," was my assertion, "that will not happen!"

"It will take a major miracle to pull me out of this one," was the rejoinder.

"O.K.," I replied. "If you need a major miracle, we will have one. My husband and I will drive in to see you. Hold on."

In an hour we were on our way, and six hours later we arrived in the young man's office. My husband was present during the conversation and since he deals in finances as a financial consultant, he sat there looking grim, shaking his head as R. related his story. Some months prior to having called me, R. had received a grant of land near a lake in that county. He, being in the real estate business, planned to build a community of lovely homes. This land had been owned by the government, and had been vacant for many years. In fact, artifacts of Indian culture were found during the excavation. Now living in this same town was an older man of Indian heritage, who was also in the real estate business. He became infuriated at the "upstart" younger man coming in and daring to build on this particular piece of land. He, of course, didn't "own" it, and had no rights whatsoever except the fact that he had lived in the community all of his life, and felt a sense of propriety on everything there. So he proceeded to go to court and sued R. for his forwardness and his daring in doing something he himself had never thought of. His charges were fraud, and they were based on such flimsy evidence, the judge threw it out of court. So with intense revenge, he went to all of the merchants and told lies about R.'s character. By this time these two court cases and the vilifying of R.'s business tactics had cost R. a great deal of money for attorneys, and R.'s credit cards were even refused at the stores. The future looked hopeless because the older man was planning a third suit.

As I listened to the story, my heart went out to the young man, but I knew that since the entire thing was based on lies it could not stand. R. also told us that a financier in Florida had been willing to loan him a million dollars for construction. "Now," he said, "that's gone."

I replied, "No way, son. We will win this situation, but you have to do your part."

"And what is that? I'm at the end of my rope," he said sadly.

"Suppose we have dinner with you and your wife this evening. Then I will lay out a method of approach to nullify this whole sordid picture. We will paint a beautiful one," I said. "In the interim, I will go to the motel and do my work of unseeing this situation. See you tonight."

By unseeing the situation, I realized that no matter how dark the picture looked, the Light of Truth could (and would) dispel it. Have you ever witnessed a sunrise? It is dark all around it but nothing—no darkness—can hold back that rising sun. It is the Light of God that never fails. Use this analogy in any condition and keep knowing that Jesus said: "Ye are the Light of the world."

We left him looking a little less pale, and certainly more hopeful. R. had been raised in a metaphysical religion, and he knew that correctly applied, it worked. That evening I told R. and his wife what they must do. "You have to spiritualize the Indian's name (incidentally, his adversary was a full-blooded Indian) and put his name in the 91st Psalm and bless him and bless him."

They both protested loudly and said, "How can we do that when he has been so awful?"

"Listen," I began, "remember what Jesus said: 'Love your enemies and pray for those who despitefully use you.' You both believe in the words of Jesus, don't you?"

7

"Yes, of course, but..."

'No buts," was my answer. "The moment you love an enemy you no longer have one."

So we spent the evening, the four of us, lifting up our concepts of the Indian, and sending him loving thoughts instead of angry ones.

I left the next day, but continued to work on the case. Two days later R. called me and said, "Guess what? The Indian walked into my office this morning, extended his hand to me, and asked me to forgive his ridiculous actions. And he dropped the third suit! So we can proceed, but I don't know about the man in Florida now."

"Call him," I answered, "and tell him you are ready for the money."

This was the result: the financier told R. that he wasn't going to send the check, but would deliver it in person. I have the newspaper clipping on R. and the Florida man signing the transaction. Anyone caring to see it may do so. It proved that one million dollars is as possible to receive as one dollar. You see, a major miracle was performed. A miracle simply means setting aside the plan of man, and putting in the Law of God.

Here are examples of letters from the alphabet that can be used to spiritualize a name:

A: Almighty, Allness, Angels
B: Beloved, Belonging, Benevolent
C: Christ-Consciousness, Control
D: Divine, Devotion
E: Eternal, Everlasting Embracing (God's Arms) Embraced
F: Fair, Father (God), Fearless
G: Grace, God, Good
H: Heaven, Harmony, Hold (fast), Haven
I: Intelligence, "I" (God's name) Inspiration, Illumine
J: Joy, Jesus, Justice
K: Knowledge, Kindness, Keenness
L: Love, Law, Liberty, Life
M: Mind, Motion, Mighty
N: Now, Noble, New
O: Omnipresent, Open, Omnipotent, Omniscient
P: Purity, Purpose, Presence
Q: Quietude, Quest
R: Resurrection, Rest, Results, Righteousness, Redeems, Right
S: Saviour, Safe, Secure
T: Truth, Triumph
U: Unity, Universal, Unfailing, Unlimited
V: Verity, Virtue, Vital-Violet (Flame Angels), Victory
W: Wisdom, Willingness, Worthiness
X: X-ray (eye of God that sees all that is real and Perfect)
Y: Yielding, You

Z: *Zero (all error is Zero), Zest*

It should be very apparent to the reader that Angels directed these people, and aided them with their great love to solve their problems so harmoniously.

A STUDENT FINDS HER WAY
(A letter from Christine Hoffman)

I was led to Poleete Carabel and the Angels at a time when every phase of my life was in absolute turmoil. I was not receiving help from the professional sources to whom I had turned (first, a psychiatrist, and then, a psychologist). I had physical problems as well that only seemed to worsen with the medical treatment I had been receiving.

The beautiful philosophies I had studied for years, and adhered to as my guide for living, proved to be nothing but frivolous words and empty thoughts when the chips were down. I found, too late, that I had built my house on sand instead of on a firm foundation as the Bible commands us to do.

Poleete Carabel and her beautiful, practical, down-to-earth teachings became my rock. She didn't just tell me that my life should be wonderful and positive, she taught me how to make it that way through metaphysical studies and the example of her own successful, joyous life.

Poleete took me very gently along the path she had trod: the inspired teachings of Christian Science, Joel Goldsmith's Infinite Way, Paramahansa Yogananda's Self-Realization, the incomparable "I Am" Teachings and her own inspired illuminations on the beloved Angels.

My so-called physical problems were handled as well, through Poleete's miraculous healing work (which, by the way, she explains she does not do, but that she is the channel for the healing which comes from God's messengers, the Masters and the Angels). I not only received help on the original problem which brought Poleete into my life, but on ailments that had plagued me intermittently since childhood.

Poleete has taught me to live a healthy, joyous and successful life, how to deal positively with whatever life hands me, and how to get a positive result every time. Through applying her teachings, especially those concerning the Angels, my life has become filled with one beautiful miracle after another.

Your life, no matter how hopeless or difficult it may seem at the moment, can become the way you want it to be, with your every constructive wish granted, if only you will read, study and incorporate the very practical teachings and examples Poleete gives in this book, into your daily living.

God bless you and keep you.

Christine Hoffman

Realization · Unity · Vision · Harmony · Joy · Discipline · Wisdom · Patience · Manifest · Gratitude · Peace · Love

Angel Bridge ™   Robinson

Chapter Two
The Bridge to the Angels

We are going to build a Bridge to the Angel World from this so-called human experience. This great and glorious project has to be made of golden planks, containing on each plank an Ideal in our consciousness, something we have to seek and live up to always.

Then we will have this tremendous Path directing us into the Angel World. They can come to us, and we can go to them, when we earn the right and fulfill each requirement. On the sides of this precious structure will be placed beautiful jewels composed of all of our good deeds and qualities.

Visualize the power of this undertaking, of what it can mean in each of your lives. You will have something tangible and real between you and the Beloved Angel World.

The Angels are always with us. But now we can enter their world of unspeakable Joy and Radiant Light. You have to earn this passage by diligence in using all of these qualities, and live them daily. Then you will be given permission to actually *become* a part of the Angel World, where only Harmony reigns, and where the Christ Presence becomes very apparent. Once having made this trek, your life will never be the same. It will be the beautiful, wondrous thing God intended it to be.

Before we experience the belief of passing on, we can enter this Holiest of Holy Angels' abodes and return to our own places in this side life filled with a glowing song in our hearts that no condition, person, or situation can ever take away. We can do this by using our God Qualities. This goal is worth every effort. Don't fail to make it yours because it will be forever!

The first plank on the Angel Bridge is *love*, the divine sense of *love* that God and Jesus have for us. *Love* is the greatest force there is in life. You cannot have anything greater. *Love* comes into your experience from everyone and everything. Think of the power of the *love* a mother has for a child, she would give up her life for it; that is the Divine Love. Receive it into your lives this moment.

The second plank on the Angel Bridge is *peace*. Without *peace* of mind, we cannot do anything. Jesus said, "My *peace* I give unto you; not as the world gives it." It has to be spiritual *peace*. And we need to send it forth into the world. The power of thought sending out *peace* could change the world. Wars start in a person's living room, and go out in ripples from there. Your thoughts are powerful. Whatever you are thinking goes forth. God gave us *peace* when He created us in His image and after His likeness, and we have forgotten it. If you have trouble stilling your mind, just keep repeating the word "God" until you feel peaceful.

Always have your thoughts on the best that life has to offer. Be careful of what you listen to and what you look at, because you can call on the Angels of *peace* when you are disturbed in your being. They are always ready and willing to give you what you need. They are always there for you; they don't leave you, you leave them.

In the Bible there are over two–hundred and forty references to the Angels. Jesus, and all of the great patriarchs, knew about the Angels. Moses used the Angels to light his way.

When you are irritated with someone, and your *peace* seems to leave you, spiritualize their name and think good thoughts about them. This can be applied to any situation you find yourself in, as well. If you are disturbed about anything, sit down and pray. When you pray, a light comes from you. *Peace* takes away the anguish of human living. This word *"peace"* is very important. You are in darkness if you don't have *peace*. You are peaceful in light. It takes light to have *peace*. In the Bible, look up the Sermon on the Mount, and the Transfiguration of Jesus. They tell you what you need to know.

The third plank on the Bridge is composed of the concept of *"the highest."* You have to live on *the highest* plane of thinking that you possibly can. You have to do that for other people, not for yourselves. Others have to put up with us, our thinking, our behavior, and the way we present ourselves to the world.

Many people think that it is not necessary to live life on *the highest* level; they swear, smoke, et cetera. They do not realize that they are creating karmic conditions that will come back to them someday. We are born in good, and we have to stay that way, or pay the debt.

It is our duty to God to stay on *the highest* plane of thought and action. Look what God has given us. We have to give something back. We all have time to be spiritual, but we have to take the time.

One way to be spiritual sounds superficial at first. But think of the concept of *the highest* when you dress yourself for the day. When you even think of Angels, you always see them beautifully clothed. You can lift people up spiritually by your appearance. Wear beautiful clear colors, and take care with your grooming. When you stay with *the highest* in all that you do, then you are walking with the Angels all of the time. They are always there. Your realization of this will attract them even closer to you.

Patience is another of the planks on your bridge. It takes *patience* to do a lot of things. We have to have *patience* with ourselves and others. We have to stand aside, have *patience*, believe and let the Angels do Their work for us.

Patience is not passivity. It takes strength to wait for God to move upon the waters. Through *patience* you get a vision of God's plan for you and for your life. At the right moment of your *patience* you get to see this. Think of the *patience* of Joseph, whose brothers were jealous of his beautiful coat of many colors. The brothers threw him in a pit, where he was found and sold into slavery. He never lost his *patience* and his love of God. He knew that God had something for him. Later he was jailed, yet he changed the thoughts of the other prisoners so that they too learned to love God. He was called before the King to interpret a dream. He foresaw seven years of plenty, and seven of famine. Food and supplies were stored up. During the famine, his brothers came before him, not realizing who he was, and asked for food. He revealed himself to them and he received them with love.

The next plank is *wisdom. Wisdom* tells us the right thing to do. *Wisdom* is intelligence, not intellect. We have to have *wisdom* to know how to proceed. God gave us *wisdom* when He created us. We can turn to the Angels and ask for the *wisdom* we need; *wisdom* and understanding.

When you ask the Angels for *wisdom,* or for anything, ask with power. Demand! Demand with power that the Angels answer your request. "I demand, Angels, that you answer my request!" If you do the right type of thinking, nothing constructive can be kept from you. It is *wisdom* to lead a decent, pure, clean life. This will give you all the power that you need.

Joy is a very important plank on the Angel Bridge. Without *joy* life would be a horrible ordeal. There is everything to be *joyous* about. Every day write down something for which you are grateful. Think of the *joy* of a small child, or of a puppy. Keep that kind of *joy* in your hearts.

Angels express nothing but *joy*. It is a little word with big meaning. When you look at a flower, you cannot help but express *joy*, because the Angels are always around flowers. Keep flowers around you; wear them, have pictures of them about you. The Angels never stop sending *joy* to us. *Joy* is everywhere. Think about the *joy* in a beautiful sunset or painting. *Joy* is in everything beautiful.

15

Vision is a plank of the Bridge to the Angels; *Vision* is not something you see with your eyes. Close your eyes and you can see a scene that you saw long ago. If you have the right sense of *inner vision*, you can improve your outer *vision*. Demand your *vision*.

Without *vision* nothing can be accomplished. We have to have the *vision* of a thing before it can come into being. The *vision* comes from inside of ourselves. That is why one need never have to wear glasses. We think we need them. But the perfect *vision* is inside you. Close your eyes and visualize what you require. Demand that the Angels bring it to you.

Realization is one plank on your Angel Bridge that you would not want to do without. *Realization* means knowing who you are. Jesus said, "Know the Truth and the Truth shall make you free." You are One with God. You are His perfect child in whom He is well pleased. *Realize* your oneness with God, with Jesus and with the precious Angels. Jesus knew of his oneness with God and gave that *realization* to everyone in His presence.

Be aware of who you really are. Be who you are. Be that spiritual idea of God. That is your true identity. Be it, live it, and don't talk about it. It is already within you. You don't have to struggle or strain to bring it forth. Jesus said, "The Kingdom of God is within." You are walking around in a kingdom. You are a king or queen. See your kingdom. Visualize it! You *do* dwell in it.

Come to the *realization* of how special you are. There is only one you through all eternity. You are an important part in God's creation and are part of everyone and everything. We are all connected to every form of life. We are One with all things. Our oneness with God is our *realization* of who we are. "I and my Father are One."

We have to love one another because we are one with even the one we don't like. So there is a part of yourself that you don't like.

God is the Knower, the Knowing and the Known. However, He does not know of your problems. He knows and *realizes* only His own creation, not yours. He created you from the fragment of His own perfect Being. *Realize* this. Know it every minute. Stay with this *realization*. It has to be lived. "You live, and move, and have your being in God."

Unity is the ninth plank on your bridge. You achieve *unity* with the Angels by building your bridge that leads to them. We need to have *unity* with all that is good and beautiful. We have to have *unity* in order to be happy. We need to *unify* ourselves with God, the Masters and the Angels. This *unity* puts us in touch with the Kingdom of God, where we already are. It also keeps us there.

Harmony is a vital golden plank. The Angel Bridge would be incomplete without it. It is important to have *harmony* in your consciousness. It is part of your being. It is there, but you have to claim it. Life is like a musical masterpiece. And we are all notes in the masterpiece of life.

Every problem in your life is caused by discordant thinking; *your* discordant thinking. Start thinking in the opposite direction. Put *harmony* in place of the discord. This is easy to do as *harmony* is always there. Don't let anxiety and fear take away your *harmony*. If you are fearful and doubting, you are not loving God. The Bible says, "Perfect love casteth out fear."

Discipline is the last plank. We must have *discipline* to not look back at our problems; to look only towards the *harmony, peace, love* and *joy*; see them and you will have them. If you keep reviewing your problems, you will have them back. We attract to us that which we focus upon.

Use *discipline* to train yourself to have power over all the wrong things. "Dis" means to separate. We need to separate ourselves from mortal, human thinking and put spiritual thinking in its place. The Angels are always with us and will always help us to do what is right. Demand that the Angels help you to have *discipline*, or whatever it is that you require.

When you complete your bridge, you can expect the Angels to use it to come to you. They are always ready with open arms to receive you. Your bridge will be a thing of beauty, and will give the precious Angels an easy access to you in every walk of your life. Soon you will find that you are entertaining Angels as constant guests and great friends. Angels are not imaginary beings; they are as real as you are, and they, too, are God's Representatives.

Chapter Three
Illumination

To illumine anything is to throw light upon it. Even an intangible idea in the mind can become tangible and real when enough illumination has been placed there. Nothing in this world would ever have been accomplished or ever would be, unless it was illumined. So this becomes a very important word in our lives.

When we use spiritual Truths to illumine our consciousness, then anything can be done. A healing takes place through illumination. An awareness of the Reality of Absolute Perfectibility comes into being and any form of disease can be eliminated; any form of lack can be filled; any fear can be cast aside. No matter what the condition calls itself, illumination reveals the Power of the Angels and shows us the love God surrounds each of us with, a light that never ceases to gleam with the life that God has given us. When you meditate deeply, you can see light even in a darkened room—"The Light of God never fails."

The instant that Love for all mankind and all things fills us, we become illuminated and everything of a discordant nature will vanish if we hold this Love. Once you feel it, don't let worldly beliefs or anything take it from you. Hold it as you would a rare jewel—protect it from the thieves of doubt, anxiety, fear, or any of the myriad beliefs that assail mankind. Let it be a garment of protection against invasion of any kind, because that illumination is the "secret place of the Most High." You are safe within it—if you will Love it and become aware of its Divine Power and blessing.

When actual photographs were taken of healers' hands with a special camera, light was definitely seen emitting from the hands—the illumination of healing Power. If they would go one step further in camera technique, the light would be violet in color, and someday they will know this. St. Germain opened the way for all who would, to see and live in these violet rays that he called "Violet Flames of Pure, Divine Love." Try surrounding your lives, your affairs, your loved ones with this violet-tinted illumination, and watch the amazing results. We know, of course, that all light comes from the sun—and those rays are violet. Put a piece of clear glass where it can receive the sun's rays, and it will become a delicate shade of violet.

Dore, a famous French artist who lived over a hundred years ago, achieved great acclaim for his paintings of Angels, and he called them "Angels of the Violet Flame." He depicted these entities as having wings. He did not realize (along with many artists who have painted Angels) that they had no wings. It was the illumination of light beams that surrounded them that gave the artists who saw them the impression that they bore wings upon their shoulders. Light is all the Angels need to propel them instantly wherever they go.

Try this experiment if you have a physical problem or an inharmonious condition of any kind. Sit quietly in meditation, pouring all the light you can manifest into the situation. Stay in the consciousness of Divine Illumination for as long as possible. If necessary, repeat this until you find the peace that is there for you.

Mrs. Eddy, the founder of Christian Science, states, "Love *designates, illumines* and *leads* the way."

Love enough, and you can accomplish anything. The Power of the Angels is in their great Love for mankind. They rejoice at being asked to help—because in the asking is a desire for the truth in the heart of the person making the request. You may not see an immediate answer, but through persistence and absolute reliance the answer will become apparent, and by asking and believing you have brought an illumination into your own awareness.

By working with this word illumination, and using it daily, you will find so many dark places of fear, anxiety, and distress disappear and your life will take on a new glow and a new meaning.

Chapter Four
Poise

Edward A. Kimball, a great metaphysician, said in an article, "Poise is our appreciation of Being." What a statement! If we can stay with this idea and be poised in every situation, we can be conquerors. Everyone has this ability—he just has to use it! Our appreciation of Being is, of course, our appreciation of Life, and since God created Life, it goes back to our appreciation of the magnitude of God. Gratitude to God must be expressed frequently during our daily life. No matter what we are doing, there's always time to pause a second and give thanks for Life. I can't say this too many times because it is so important. Take the time occasionally to sit down and write on paper all the things for which you are really grateful.

I knew a woman who had been in a serious accident. So many bones in her body were broken that the doctors did not set any of them because she was not expected to live. Her step-daughter called me as Marian, my friend, asked her to do. I went immediately to the hospital in Oxnard where she had been taken, and against the doctor's advice and orders, I had her moved to a Christian Science Sanitarium. In two weeks, she was home and healed. That dear one told me that she even expressed gratitude for the sheets on her bed, for her pillow, for the straw through which she drank and for everything she could see and think of. No wonder her healing came so fast! God has given us the Gift of Life, and it must be cherished. We can't take it for granted. You might think, "But there are so many, many people, how can *I* be special?" But you are. Each one is an

Idea of God's Creation, and it takes all of us to make up the whole. We reflect God as a sunbeam reflects the sun. Every sunbeam is an important part of the sun. When you even just think of the word poise, you know that Angels certainly are always aware of it and are always ready to help us attain that in our lives.

Chapter Five
I Corinthians Chapter 13
Spiritual Interpretation (Charity)

Spiritual Interpretation of
I Corinthians
Chapter 13
This book from the Bible was written by St. Paul

1.   "Though I speak with the tongues of men and of angels, and have not charity, I am became as sounding brass, or a tinkling cymbal."

The word charity has more or less relegated itself to meaning charitable institutions entirely, or charitable people who give money or things to the needy. This is one connotation of the word, but by no means the important one. Charity has to begin in the heart. It means leniency and brotherly love. The word leniency interested me, as I pondered it, because I saw that it covered a great deal of territory in our lives. We must be lenient toward everyone, and unless we are, we could not feel brotherly love. And of course, we come to that important word, "forgiveness"—if we are lenient towards another we must forgive—whatever we think we see or whatever we think we have been through at the hands of another, we must replace it with Love.

2.   "And though I have the gift of prophecy, and understand all mysteries, and all knowledge; and though I have all faith, so that I could remove mountains, and have not charity, I am nothing."

3.   "And though I bestow all my goods to feed the poor and though I give my body to be burned and have not charity, it profiteth me nothing."

"Charity suffereth long and is kind; charity envieth not, charity vaunteth not itself, is not puffed up; doth not behave itself unseemly; seeketh not her own; is not easily provoked; thinketh no evil; rejoiceth not in iniquity, but rejoiceth in the truth."

4.   "Beareth all things, believeth all things, hopeth all things, endureth all things."

Paul has propounded meaning after meaning to charity, feeling that charity was the most important word in our lives.

When he states "believeth all things," I'm certain he means only those things that have a spiritual value. A great leader in metaphysics states, "An acknowledgment of the perfection of the Infinite Unseen confers a Power nothing else can."

The statement "endureth all things" does not mean that we should become floor mats to be walked on—it means by enduring (to hold on to the Truth) to live it—to be it! And always to be filled with hope (not a weak sense of just hoping for good) but knowing that we are "heirs to the Kingdom."

5.   "Charity never faileth but whether there be prophecies, they shall fail; whether there be tongues, they shall cease; whether there be knowledge, it shall vanish away."

6.   "For we know in part, and we prophesy in part."

Paul is speaking of false prophesy, which seems to be pretty rampant these days. Every person who even thinks he is a psychic is foretelling future events that never occur. He says Charity never faileth, and in order to pray correctly we must have charity to the fullest extent. True prayer can turn the tide of anything. I have witnessed this hundreds of times in my life. I have seen conditions change in a matter of minutes. We could call a doctor's verdict a kind of prophecy.

I have seen these verdicts turn completely, even when the death sentence was given as a final declaration. Prayer changed the condition into Life and health.

Paul says that we only know in part anyway. If we do not see the Truth, the *spiritual Truth* of anything, we are only knowing a very small part of Life.

7.   "But when that which is perfect is come, then that which is in part shall be done away."

When we become conscious of Perfection in our lives, not looking at the appearance but seeing "righteous judgment," then the so-called imperfect part will vanish.

8.   "When I was a child, I spake as a child, I understood as a child, I thought as child, but when I became a man, I put away childish things."

He is, of course, is speaking about emotional immaturity. And many suffer with this ailment, which has nothing to do with years. But as we develop in understanding, the immature thinking is erased, and we rise to our true being in God.

9.   "For now we see through a glass darkly; but then face to face: Now I know in part; but then shall I know even as also I am known."

In other words, before we mature in consciousness to the realization of Light, we see only the dark side of things—the problems that we think can't be solved—the so-called tragedies of the world. But when we face a situation armed with the knowledge that every problem has a solution—no matter what it is—and out of what was called a tragedy, some greatness appeared. We are now beginning to really *know* God as He knows us—as His beloved children. Never, never forget that God loves you because you are His own.

10.   "And now abideth faith, hope, charity, these three; but the greatest of these is Charity."

Faith based upon understanding; hope filled with the realization of God's allness, charity. The greatest fraught with complete surrender of self—and overflowing with Love.

Compassion

Compassion is a beautiful word, and has many lovely connotations. Everyone loves a truly compassionate person. Many times throughout this book "we" (me, myself and I) have said that the little ego of personal self has to be completely eliminated—blasted out, in other words. How do you do this? By constantly thinking of other people besides yourself—not wasting valuable time on frivolous things or thoughts.

One of the happiest, most contented people I have ever met spent four to five hours every day in Cedars of Lebanon Hospital attending the sick and bedridden. She received no payment in money for this (fortunately, she was married to a successful man) but her real, permanent payment came in the joy she brought to others. She wasn't necessarily what one might call a religious person, as far as a church went. But, she had the spirit of love which was the most beautiful thing she could have possessed. Her face always glowed with happiness because she was "living" the Christ-like life (even if, being of Jewish origin, she was unaware of it). She came to me for healings, and we had many beautiful experiences. We didn't talk much about my procedure. I just put my hands on her, and realized her perfection in God's Beloved Kingdom. She responded every time, and never questioned me one way or another. She just accepted, which was a very childlike thing to do. She expected a healing, so she received one.

Jesus said, "Behold I have set before thee an open door." I have mentioned this before, but not fully. To behold means to hold on to your real Being, which is the "Child of God." And this dear lady walked through that "open door" and I beheld her real being. This was having compassion in spite of her former training and so-called "opposite" beliefs. In my thinking, I erased all of those and saw only the perfection that was her birthright. The Bible states, "Ye are heirs to the Kingdom of God and joint-heirs with Christ." In all of my healing works, I do this same thing. I do not allow the erroneous condition or situation to occupy my thinking, because if God in His image and likeness (and He did) made man, then we have to see everyone that way. This is compassion.

I saw an example of true compassion on television a few days ago. It was on the "Oprah Winfrey Show." Oprah is a beautiful woman, whose face shines with compassion for everyone. Tears ran down her lovely face while one of the visitors in the audience was telling about a very sad incident in her life. I've seen and heard many talk–show hosts, but never have I witnessed anyone who showed real feelings before. I also saw Oprah draw a young girl to her and comfort her after she had related a sorrowful story. Oprah Winfrey isn't afraid to also state her beliefs about God and spiritual things. This, to me, is true greatness and true love. She deserves any merit she might receive, because she isn't just saying words of compassion, she is living them.

It is simple to use words like "I'm sorry for them," et cetera, but are you doing something about it? If you cannot do anything physical, you can at least pray for that person or condition. My dear mother, God bless her, always said to me, never turn anyone down who comes to your door and needs help. "At least," she used to say, "let them stay on your porch while you fix them something to eat." It is, of course, not wise to invite a stranger into your house, but don't send them away empty-handed; show your compassion for mankind. It takes so little time, and the rewards are great because it makes your heart feel good.

Some of the meanings of the word "compassion" are (from the thesaurus): consideration, fellow–feeling, tenderness, forbearance, mercy, clemency, leniency, enter into the feelings of, be kind, appeal to one's better self, and tender hearted. I related to all of these. The one, "enter into the feelings of," reminded me of an old Native American proverb: "Never judge a man until you have walked a mile in his moccasins." This is such a true statement, because people are prone to judge another person harshly for a mistake—or for a condition in his or her life. You cannot do that. Even if you are not on a spiritual path–acting purely human, you should stop and think, "What if I were going through the same situation—how would I behave?" If you are on a spiritual path, you could ask yourself, "What would Jesus do under these circumstances?" The answer would always be, "Have compassion and love." I have worked this way dozens of times and the answer was always right.

Awareness

To have awareness is "to be cognizant of; to realize." Another meaning, which I thought was interesting, is, "to be watchful." This is an important word, because if we are watchful of what we do, what we think, then fewer mistakes would be made humanly and spiritually. It is the moment of unwatchfulness that makes a person angry, or even impatient. If one would stop and think before speaking in a temper, or even with impatience, a great deal of misunderstandings could be avoided between people in business, with children, and between married couples.

Awareness is one of the most important facets in one's character, for without it a person can be not only dull, but very self-centered. A man may be keenly aware of things that go on outwardly around him, and be aware of his own feelings, ambitions, and desires, but unaware completely of anyone else that he contacts. True, the average person cannot see the inside workings of another, but he should try, with understanding, to realize the traumas and even heartaches of another.

Ben, my husband, was telling me the other day how his mother was complaining about those poor Vietnamese people that were brought over here for succor from the communists who invaded their country. He asked her how she would feel if she were one of them, and he said, "Wouldn't you be grateful if another country gave you refuge and help?" Of course her answer was "Yes." She had been unaware of the situation until her son straightened her out.

We must be aware of others all over the world. Our love has to be inclusive. Everyone can develop an awareness. First of all, you must start with an awareness of God, the Power of the Angels, and the Christ Consciousness. With that, you open up a whole new world as you pray and meditate deeply for this spiritual awareness; other marvelous things will follow. Suddenly you find yourself being aware of your brothers' needs and wanting to help fulfill them.

When you really become aware of life, as being completely spiritual, you have opened a door that has been closed for perhaps centuries. Jesus said, "Knock and it shall be opened unto you." Awareness is that knocking at the door of consciousness. Suddenly, the light streams in and makes all things new. The true nature of God, His Great and Glorious plan for man, dawns upon the awakened thought.

Then one really realizes his place in the mighty scheme of things, and sees himself as an integral part of the whole. He then knows the role he must play—to love, to be unselfish, to forgive (Jesus said, "Seventy times unto seventy.").

Did it ever occur to you that God is always aware of each of you individually? Not as sick, sinful mortals, but as Divine Ideas filled with light, reflected back to Him in the same perfection He possesses. If this were not so, a healing could never take place. The healer must behold and see only perfection.

Awareness means to be alive. To have awareness—awareness of oneself as a spiritual Idea—makes any achievement possible, no matter how impossible it might look or seem. What made a man like Luther Burbank accomplish the apparently impossible? His awareness of the Christ Principle in his life.

I read an account about Luther Burbank from a book by Baird T. Spaulding. Mr. Spaulding had known Mr. Burbank from the time he was six years old. This is what Mr. Spaulding relates from first-hand knowledge:

"One Sunday afternoon, Luther walked with his father to visit a neighbor. They took a shortcut through the fields and passed through a potato patch. As children will do, little Luther ran ahead. It was at the time when the potato blooms were ripening. One stem was standing up a little higher than the others and Luther stopped to look at it, and his father said that when he came up the flower was waving back and forth. The boy said to him, 'Papa, it's talking to me.' 'Well,' the father told my father, 'I thought the boy was going daft, so I took his hand and hurried over to the neighbor's.' All the time they were there, Luther was anxious to return and finally, after half past three, they started homeward. They returned through the same potato field. The boy rushed ahead and went directly to the same potato plant. There was a great calm over the field, not a leaf stirred. When the father came up to where the boy was standing, that tall seed pod was moving again, back and forth. And Luther said, 'Papa, I want to stay here. Jesus is talking to me and telling me what to do.' His father took him right home, made him do his chores, and sent him to bed. In a short while he found him tiptoeing downstairs trying to get out of the house. He was sent back to bed three different times that night. By that time it was eleven o'clock and his parents thought he was sound asleep for the night.

"The next morning, Luther was missing. The father instinctively walked out into the field and there he found Luther wrapped around that potato pod, just as close as he could get to it, sound asleep. When he was awakened, he said, 'Papa, Jesus talked with me all night long and He told me that if I would watch that little bulb until it ripened, take it and plant the seed next spring, that when it developed, there would be one potato there that would make me famous.'" And that is just what happened!

You see, Luther became aware of the Christ Consciousness and that awareness led him throughout his life. He listened and obeyed the voice that spoke to him. You, too, have these marvelous gifts within you, but you must become conscious of them, and meditate deeply for the answer. The Angels are always ready and willing to guide and direct your way.

Understanding
"Judge not that ye be not judged."

If we truly have understanding, we would never judge anyone for any-thing. We can't sit in the seat of judgment on another, because we never know what caused the person or persons to act or do the things they do. True, we cannot condone wrong actions, but we must try to understand. Certainly I do not condone this rash of non-married couples living together, but I do understand it. Can any of you tell me what you think it is?

It's mass hypnotism. It has grown out of woman's desire to be "free," as they call it. What is real freedom? Certainly not disobeying the law of the land and the law of God. That isn't freedom—that is bondage, because these people are binding themselves with Karma for many lives to come. A woman is the spiritual leader, or should be, in any situation. When she breaks down the moral code, most men (practically all of them) don't object. Young men now are talking about freedom, too. This women's lib thing is going to backfire on women as sure as I'm sitting here. I've seen it start in the younger people already.

We who are on a spiritual path should *not condone* anything that takes femininity from a woman. I heard that a law was passed to allow women to engage in any kind of male sport. Again, this is definitely hyp-notic. Imagine a woman playing football among men! Women were not created for this sort of rough sport. Women were created to be mothers and to be women.

I sincerely feel that a woman should help financially when she can in marriage. But don't take the manhood away from men by not letting them open a car door, or placing a chair for you at the table—missing the little courtesies that go with a man being a man and a woman being a woman. This is the lack of understanding. God made us all in *His* image and likeness, that is true. A woman expresses the womanhood of God, and a man the manhood of God, making a whole unit and yet each being an individual to serve individual purposes.

Volumes could be written on this word, *understanding*, because in all walks of life, we must have it in order to live a spiritual existence. With-out it, one becomes selfish and self-centered.

When Solomon was told by God that he could have any gift he desired, he asked not for riches or fame, but wisdom and understanding. He received the riches, but he also became one of the wisest men of all Bible history. And he became dedicated to God. He was aware of Angel Power, and filled his temple with replicas of Angels.

Let us look for a moment at what the word "understanding" really means. Breaking it down, it means "substance." "Sub" means "under"—"stance" means "standing." They speak of the substance of an idea, the care of an idea or the understanding of an idea. Also, a man of substance has wealth beneath his feet, which gives him a certain amount of human power, because feet placed on anything gives one dominion over it. He has dominion over lack, and the power to buy what he pleases.

Even by *understanding* fully the Law of Supply, we need not lack for anything. What is that law? It is the complete realization that we are heirs to the Kingdom of God, and as heirs, we inherit all good—but we must claim this inheritance.

Every demonstration over any form of lack—lack of health, lack of companionship, or lack of money—has to be made first by believing, and then by understanding that God is the *one and only power* and, as we draw upon this, we receive that power into our lives.

Any form of human material thinking adulterates *understanding* completely. Faith in anything but God, the Angels and the Christ Consciousness takes us off the pinnacle of power and puts us into the mire of materiality, and places our feet on sand instead of the Substance of a firm foundation.

Man wonders, when he allows himself to be blown by every wind or circumstance, why his life is so mixed–up and is filled with so many unsolved problems. He blames his parents or his wife or his boss—when all the time he himself is bringing the condition into his own life. It only takes an instant to true understanding to change any situation in the "twinkling of an eye." I have witnessed this many, many times.

Mary Baker Eddy, in *Science and Health*, states: "Understanding is the line of demarcation between the real and the unreal." The real is perfection...the unreal is "Maya" or illusion. When a healing (it should be called a "revealing") takes place, perfection is seen to manifest in the so-called problem. You might think that the material condition has been changed, but *actually* and *spiritually* there is no material condition because matter does not really exist as *all* is Mind or God in action.

God is All-Knowing, but He only knows the *real*, which is perfect. If God, with His All-Knowing Mind, knew any condition of imperfection, it would be real and there would be nothing you or I could do about it. How did Jesus heal? By beholding the Perfect Man or the Perfect Condition—then it was manifested. When spiritual Truths are accepted into one's consciousness as the *only* reality, then the power of that truth nullifies the erroneous pictures and presents the perfection that was always there.

The energy behind Truth is spiritual, and no material concepts can remain when one is armed with its power, majesty, *understanding*. Spiritual realization annihilates the material concepts. This has been proven thousands of times.

Again I quote from Mrs. Eddy: "*Understanding* changes the stand-

31

points of life from a material to a spiritual basis." So, in order to function as a spiritual person, we must strive for *understanding*. I have people tell me that they are spiritual. What they really mean is that they would *like* to be. No one is truly even on a spiritual path, until he follows the dictates of an absolutely pure life to the letter—pure from malice, from envy, from moodiness, from judging, from fear, and from hate in any form. Again we see that *understanding* plays a most important role in our spiritual endeavors.

Synonyms for the word "understanding," according to the dictionary, are reason, intelligence, intuition and judgment. When we reason together, we come closer to one another and a greater bond of mutual understanding develops. If married couples would sit down and reason out their differences, many divorces could be avoided. Intelligence also plays a large part in being able to see another's viewpoint because intelligence, based upon understanding, can solve almost any problem. Then, to be able to see intuitively into the heart of a condition or situation is of primary importance. Some people are born with intuition. Those who are not can definitely achieve it through deep meditation.

With intuition, our judgment can always be correct, because it will be based upon an understanding of who and what we really are. We then become capable of using *the great God Power* that we all possess, and must learn again to use. Demand audibly that you have this power and that you will know how to use it. Don't be afraid to ask audibly for the ability to make this power available at the instant you need it. The more you do this, the greater will be your *understanding* of what life is really all about.

Chapter Six
Karma, the Law of Cause and Effect

The word "Karma" is not understood by many people, and yet to understand what it really means is perhaps one of the most important concepts we can possibly have. Karma explains the "why" of so many, many puzzling aspects of life. In the Bible, Saint Paul states in his epistles, "As ye sow, so shall ye reap." This is the law of Karma. Once a person has created the law of Karma, as he does with every act and thought, he will be either rewarded or punished, as the case may be. God does not do this. Karma was created by man himself as a balance wheel. He must therefore accept the fact that he has to be born again and again upon the earth, because this is the only place, through a material body, that one can learn and ultimately return to the Source.

Karma has to be understood spiritually. Human reason will try to rule it out, but it stands, regardless of the arguments against it, as a fact. How can a Mozart, for instance, be explained, who composed sonatas at the age of five, without ever having had a single lesson in music? He had to have been reincarnated from another life, and brought over, to the one he lived. Then in the present time, there was a little Korean boy of six who spoke five languages and completely "stumped" the leading physicists with his knowledge of calculus. He could solve problems faster than the greatest mathematician and did it with ease. I saw him perform on television. How could anyone doubt that this little child had lived before as some noted scientist?

There are children born blind and crippled and mentally retarded. Why? Because somewhere, sometime in another life's experience, they had done something that gave them a Karmic debt to pay in this life. True, we have to have the greatest compassion for these people. Our duty and privilege is to help them when we can. We do not judge. We love and pray for them all. Many people, religious ones at that, call these conditions the will of God. What a terrible thing to say or believe. God would have to be a cruel monster to allow this. God is a God of Love. He sends His "Angels to have charge over us" and to help us in all our ways. God only knows the Light of His Own Being. He created us in perfection, but mankind using his free-will, went against the Creator and became greedy, selfish, unkind and war-like—so man himself created Karma. In other words, man disturbed the harmony and beauty of his own being and must therefore pay the debt to the fullest.

The law of Karma is impersonal, being the servant of its creator—man. There have been, and still are great spiritually enlightened people who can consciously control the forces of Karma. For instance, healers can help people adjust their lives and avert certain Karmic conditions. But the ability to do this for others takes deep meditation and unselfish dedication on the part of the healer. It cannot be achieved by wishing for it or in using a desultory hit-and-miss approach to spiritual awareness. It takes understanding and also love. We all have access to this power, but very few people ever work to attain it.

Doing good for the sake of applause or plaudits, such as a rich man donating a park or building to gain favor, does not affect the Karmic Law in the least. It might have good outer effects, but good deeds have to be done from the heart, and in silence, then the benefactor reaps rewards and this helps to discard bad Karma from his life. However, good deeds and actions do not go unrewarded completely if the motive and "intent of the heart" is pure, even if they are made public. (Katherine Kulman, for instance, was an example of this. Her great healing ministry was certainly publicly lauded, but her motive of unself was very evident in everything she did.)

Hour by hour, we are choosing our direction, and the Law, with absolute justice, acts accordingly. "Life becomes what it does." These words are really the essence of Karma.

Human history is a record of the Karma of humanity; working itself out according to the good or evil of our racial, national or personal needs. Materlink, the author of the *Blue Bird*, and many other famous works, said, "Let us remember that nothing befalls us that is not of the nature of ourselves."

We actually possess nothing, because when we leave this earthly plane, we can't take a thing with us, not even our human bodies. The only thing a man can call his own is *what he does, and how he thinks*. Man is punished by his sins—not for them. And, in the opposite direction, he is re-

34

warded by his good deeds—not for them. Karma itself neither rewards nor punishes; it only restores the balance of lost harmony. He who suffers deserves the suffering, and he who has reason to rejoice is reaping what he has sown.

But remember, once again I say, even if those sufferers caused their own condition, there is absolutely no excuse for being heartless or callous toward their suffering. We must try to help wherever and whenever we can. If not physically, then we must pray for those less fortunate than ourselves. It is a Law of Mystical Dynamics that a given amount of energy expended on a spiritual plateau is far more productive in results than the same amount based on the material, or physical plane. So, prayers based on love have power to help the suffering.

Once Karma is fully understood, it will be seen that there is no such thing as good or bad luck, and there is definitely no such thing as fate. Fate would imply a blind power. But man is a free agent. He creates his own life. There have been many who have risen above terrible handicaps. For instance, an artist who became completely paralyzed. She paints by holding the brush between her teeth. It takes her two–and–a half months to draw a picture, but she earns a living that way. I also read of a paraplegic who runs a big business and employs many people. These people are working out their Karma in a courageous way and rising above their problems.

We have but one excuse for our bondage, that we lack the will to be free. If there is no luck or chance, there is no such thing as coincidence. However amazing the so-called happening might seem to be, each set of facts was the result of previous causes or acts. The many, many stories people (who by an amazing series of events are drawn to a particular place or away from it at the moment a terrible event takes place) are not accidental or coincidental. For some reason, that person was meant to be at a given place, at a given time when the tragedy took place, or were saved from being there by other situations. Such as a friend of mine who missed a plane by only three minutes that crashed and killed all of those aboard.

Madame Blavatsky, founder of Theosophy, said, "Karma explains the inequities and inequalities of daily life. Only Karma can explain the mysterious problem of good and evil and reconcile man to the terrible apparent injustice of life. Only the knowledge of Karma alone prevents man from cursing life and other men, as well as their Creator."

Nothing is more untrue than the words "all men are equal." That would be impossible. Each is born with the burden, pleasant or unpleasant, of his own past life Karma. And no two men are equal; for no two men are the same. Everyone knows that there are no identical fingerprints. All souls were created at the same time, but each person is an absolute individual every time he is reborn.

We are aware that all of mankind is of one family, whatever the color or race, but the members are of different time periods. Therefore, there can be no equality of opportunities or responsibilities. Although everyone is marching toward the same goal (whether he knows it or not), he cannot carry the same burdens as another. Each of our so-called burdens, heavy or light, have been earned in another past life.

Karma expresses not that which a man inherits from his ancestors, but that which he inherits from himself in some pervious state of existence. In the same way, environment is a product of one's own past actions for each new birth brings new Karma to live out in the present experience or repeat in another incarnation.

The person being re-embodied chooses his own parents, and the body that those particular parents would provide for the working out of past Karma. Heredity is the servant of Karma, not its substitute.

If it were not for conflicts that breed hatred and strife, Karma would never have a weapon or force to work through. These conflicts start in one's own household, and spread out until they become war. Each war only attracts another one. There will never be a war to end all wars, except the warfare with one's self to learn how to discipline one's life and thinking into love and harmony. If man will slay the foe within his own consciousness, and refuse to judge another or to hate in any way, he will find the "peace that passeth all understanding." Then when he has done a thorough enough job on himself, he can go forth armed with the truth he has learned, with great efforts, and help his fellow man to learn the same lesson.

The advantages of working by the Law of Karma are multitudinous. The Law gives a reason for right living. It proves that it pays dividends to be honest, loving and unselfed. It reveals a world of consciousness where right becomes the real reason for being, and a man must do right not because it rewards, but because he is impelled to by his own conscience.

We must constantly realize that we are "our brothers' keepers." Only by the light of complete compassion and an understanding love for all that lives, can one see clearly that Karma, as a Law, is actually a loving Law, that it is just and places a person, if he will but heed, in a position to realize that he must change in order to improve his life pattern.

I have a very dear friend, Nancy, who is perhaps one of the kindest, loveliest people I have ever met, but her entire life, from the beginning, has been a shambles. When she came to me for a "reading" some years ago, I saw her great need. She was married to an alcoholic; a good man, basically; he earned a good living but he drank constantly. This made life very miserable for her and her children. Then she told me that her father and mother were alcoholics, and so were her sister and brother. She had been reared in that atmosphere, and finally married into it also, unwittingly, at the age of eighteen. When I first met her, I asked her about religion. "Oh, I gave that all up," she answered. "It was useless. My life is too miserable to be able to think straight."

"Go back home," I insisted. "Get out your books again. Start going

36

to church, and I will help you."

Nancy did as I asked her to do, and she was very happy for awhile in her religion. She served in the church and kept busy. She took advanced classes in Metaphysics, and where the outward picture in her home had not changed, she still was content within herself. In a few years her husband passed on from drinking.

Nancy met another man some time later and soon they were married. He joined her church and put on a beautiful act of being a dutiful husband, but he was a compulsive gambler, and spent all of his time at the race track. He suffered heavy financial losses. Nancy divorced him after a few months. She met another man, who also joined her church. In every respect he seemed the right one, but his son was a dope addict, and caused endless problems in their home. Soon this husband became an alcoholic and was very abusive. Nancy once again forgot her religion in the midst of all the human problems. She came to me one day in great desperation. I hadn't seen her for almost a year. Once again, I placed her feet on a spiritual path. We prayed for her husband and he was receptive enough to put himself in a hospital for the cure of alcoholism.

This time Nancy seems to be staying on the path completely. She has learned that there is no other answer for anything. This whole situation is the result of Karma, that is for sure, if I ever saw one.

Nancy is capable of reaching great heights spiritually. She has even seen Angels. So she knows their power, but through many, many lives she has deviated from the path of Light; gone into a complete human way of thinking and living and has had to suffer these Karmic situations over and over. The higher we are capable of going, if we falter, the greater the suffering.

My constant prayer is that Nancy will keep walking Godward in this life so that her next one will be as beautiful as she is.

I sincerely hope that I have made this chapter on Karma clear. I have written it as simply as I could. The subject is a profound one and few understand it—or don't want to, would be a better way to say it. The human mind wants to have someone or something to blame for what befalls it in life. But by knowing that we are the masters of our own circumstances, only then can we rise and conquer all obstacles. The power of Angels is always there to lift and to help and make life a wonderful thing.

Chapter Seven
Reincarnation

The meaning of the word "Re" means to turn back or come back. "Incarnation" means in a material body. So the entire word means to return in a human form after one has passed on. The time element of this varies. Sudden deaths usually mean a fast return within a few years, and upon occasions it has been recorded, within a few months.

This is a documented, true happening. It occurred some time ago. At the age of six, little Elsie died. The grief of her parents was inconsolable. During the life of Elsie she had a French nurse, who taught her to speak French and to sing several songs in that language. Some months after Elsie had passed, her mother found that she was pregnant. One night the mother dreamed that Elsie appeared to her and said, "Mommie, I am the baby you are carrying. I will be born again to you and Daddy."

The mother related the dream to her husband and they both decided that it was only wishful thinking. However, when the child was born, it was a girl and looked exactly like Elsie, but once again they put it down as coincidence, but they did name the new baby Elsie. As she grew, her mannerisms and actions became identical to that of their dead child. Again they believed it to be just an accidental happening. This new Elsie did not have the French nurse, but an English girl came to care for her. One day when Elsie was about three, her mother heard her singing in a strange tongue. She called her and had her repeat the song. It was the same one that Elsie had learned in her other life from the French nurse. Then the mother knew that her dream had been a reality.

There are countless cases recorded that absolutely prove reincarnation. I have perused many of them. Yet in spite of proof, many people do not believe it. I sincerely think that it is because they do not understand the whys and wherefores of reincarnation. It actually is the only logical explanation of life. We all know that God is a God of love and justice, and yet there appears to be so many inequalities in life in general. Conditions surrounding people living on the same street can be so diametrically opposite. One child will be born perfectly normal while another just a block away is born blind and crippled. What is the explanation? It has to be a Karmic condition carried over from another incarnation. Now if the child born blind and crippled is given a spiritual education, and he seeks it diligently, he can be perfectly normal at his next rebirth.

The search for a right understanding of God is absolutely essential. God is the Source and the original creator of Perfect Man, but He gave man free-will and man misused it (in most cases to his detriment) so he must struggle to once more attain his original status with God and eventually return to the Source.

Some people go through hundreds and perhaps thousands of incarnations, clawing their way, until spiritual awakening comes. I have seen people who have lived sensual, material lives, who, a few months prior to their passing, literally come begging for some of life's truths. One case in particular was a man who lived completely in sensual pleasure for many years. Without his being aware of it, his wife and I had prayed many times for him and he had received some miraculous healings. One was a complete mental breakdown. The doctors were ready to give him shock treatments. He actually asked for help this time, during a lucid moment, and he was completely healed. He pursued his law practice for several more years. He forgot about his healing, however, and continued his drinking and loose living. A year later he had a stroke and was "healed" again. This man, whose name was Max, came to me and asked to study Metaphysics. He was a very apt student and made a complete metamorphosis. He passed a year later, but he had sought the Truth, so his passing was an easy one, and his rebirth will probably be into a much healthier and better life than he knew before.

It has been my privilege to witness, during my years in the healing works (and also during my entrance into the past lives of many people) that I have been able to see a reasonable answer for all problems that seem to beset mankind. I attempt to pass this knowledge on to those who are receptive and willing to receive it, thereby solving problems that would seem insurmountable.

After a regression, I have beheld a complete change of personality in people, and an ability not only to overcome, but to cope with serious situations that otherwise might have caused traumatic conditions that could have proved fatal in some instances. Opening up the Akashic Records and going back into other incarnations has thus been of great aid to those who need it. The Akashic Records are secret documents hidden from the average person. Only a Mystic who has spent his or her life in a powerful spiritual metaphysical study can do this. These amazing documents contain the complete story of everyone's life on this earth and their past lives. Every Karmic condition, good or bad, is revealed.

This particular system of unveiling the mysteries that can lie deeply hidden, and yet plague one's present life to an almost unbelievable degree, is done in cases where I feel it is necessary or where I know the one receiving can benefit by the regression. Some of the remarkable things I have seen recorded have actually amazed *me*, whom I thought was beyond amazement. In many instances, when I received names and dates, I refer people to the library to look up the incidents. In every case they have proven remarkably correct, even to descriptions of appearance in other lives. In the case of my husband, for instance, I received absolutely accurate data on two of his last lives on this plane. I like to have the person research for himself and find data correct that had been revealed to me.

Many people say that the Bible does not teach reincarnation so it can't be true. However, this is not factual. There are references made by Jesus himself that prove it. For instance, he said, "Before Abraham was I am." Jesus made no idle statements. What did this mean? How could anyone decipher another connotation to this statement except that He had lived before?

In ancient Bibles, reincarnation was given great play, but when the Byzantine Justinian became emperor in or about 55 a.d., he had all the references he could find removed from the Bible. He didn't understand it because of his ignorance so he used his power to have reincarnation taken out of the text. This has been proven by Bible scholars who researched the old Bibles and found that reincarnation was a very profound subject taught in all of them.

As one learns to understand reincarnation he becomes more aware of and more understanding of God's great love and wisdom. God did not create Karma, man did this for himself.

How could any intelligent thinking person ever doubt the facts behind reincarnation when a regression is so possible? Yet there are "diehards" who claim it is against God. The very opposite is true. The knowledge that you can make your lives better brings you ever closer to the Source, which is God. God has given each of us the "gift of Life" and we have a choice to appreciate that gift by living on a high plane, or casting aside the "gift" and letting the lower instincts take over. You are given chance after chance. Take it, use it wisely, and learn to love more. To love is the secret key to Life; not the physical connotations of love, but true, God-like love. This love forgives, blesses, and with great appreciation to the Divine Presence, pours forth constant gratitude for each life that you are given, to correct and improve so that someday you will be worthy enough to sit at the

"Right Hand" of God! This is earth's preparatory school—use it to the utmost by learning how to live—with Angels.

Chapter Eight
Self-discipline

First of all, we have to eliminate the small "I" or little self, because selfishness is not only a disease, it is the greatest sin of man. Most people put fences around themselves and their families and dwell in this narrow space. Everything they do, every thought they have, goes right back to the self. In this crowded space there is no room for expansion of any kind, especially spiritual expansion, which is the most important one of all.

Hundreds of people come to me for help, and in every case—with few exceptions—whether the problem is emotional, physical, or financial, it has to do with the self-interest of the person. I don't sit in judgment or condemnation—my only feeling is love and a desire to help each individual to extricate himself or herself from this bond of self into a higher consciousness.

The Self-hood of God can only be learned when we eliminate the "little–self" fences and look out and see other people, because these fences really become high walls and they block out the light to such a degree that one becomes blinded to everyone else but his "own." Actually, nothing is your own because we own absolutely nothing—certainly not our families. We chose to "borrow" them for this life and our children chose to "borrow" us. No matter how many millions of dollars a man has, he doesn't own a cent of it. Could poor Aristotle Onassis take any of his money with him? No, of course not. Those millions are being fought over now by his heirs. Of course, he had use of the money while he was here, but what a life he led—a very sad one—seeking and seeking to grab a little happiness humanly, but never really succeeding. Only those who contribute to mankind's good find real joy and happiness because they are living out of the little "self."

One doesn't have to be a Luther Burbank or Paramahansa Yogananda, or anyone of fame. He can live out of this self right where he is. It has to start within the heart, and a desire to reach out and help. As we do what seems to be the simple selfless things, greater opportunities arise to do more.

This is where self-discipline comes in, when we are faced with circumstances that take great love, dedication, and no human judgment whatsoever. To see each one as we want to be seen.

Anger over anything is not only belittling to the one getting angry—it is a barrier to spiritual progress and keeps one down on a low level. Impatience does the same thing. Jesus always expressed the greatest tolerance. Even when Judas betrayed him, he did not become angry or impatient. He knew that this was Judas' Karma. And Jesus was rewarded by ascending into the heavenly kingdom. He loved greatly, so he tempered all of his judgments with this love.

On the other hand, Moses, who labored to lead the children of Israel out of bondage, knew that he did not love enough. He allowed his sense of the Law to take precedence over everything and actually he broke the Law by putting to death those who worked on the Sabbath. He broke the Law of "Thou shalt not kill." So he was never to be allowed in the promised land. The Israelites, on the other hand, had bowed down and worshipped the golden calf, so they had to wander for forty years in the desert with great privations.

So do many people worship false gods, particularly the god of the little ego—self. They also worship money, possessions, et cetera. Oh, they may go to a church every week, but they are not living up to any real religion except their own false concepts. We must use self-discipline (the higher God–Self) to meditate daily and to give forth what we have to give.

As in the Biblical story of Elijah and the widow woman, when Elijah asked for something to eat, she told him she has only one cruse of oil but that she would share it with him. She gave of what she had, and from then on the cruse never became empty. As we give freely and joyfully of whatever it may be, our oil will be replenished and running over. Make of yourself a channel for the good to flow into your lives. Discipline your thinking and your acting.

Every single element of life and living can be accomplished by determination and self-discipline. No one needs to grow old, no one needs to lack, or to be sick. The barriers that hold back complete realization are within the person himself—never, never outside. On the other hand, the ability to think and to know has been given to all. Lethargy must be overcome with a firm resolve to allow no negativity to ever come into the thinking. Think perfection, and work to attain it in every department of life.

God has endowed man with great and magnificent powers, but they must be used constantly and with gratitude given to the Divine Father for the gifts He has given us. Self-discipline is the key word to life and living. Without it man is blown by every wind of circumstance and arrives no place.

Take your life in your own hands and make something beautiful out of it. Determine to do this with self-discipline. Go forth armed with love for all mankind, with the complete knowledge that we are put here for one purpose, to give joyously and freely–and as we do this selflessly, we earn the reward of true happiness within our beings.

Talk to your Angels when you feel the need of more self-discipline in your life. Keep remembering that God gave them "charge over you in all your ways."

Chapter Nine
Consciousness

To be conscious of something is to be aware of it. When you are studying a metaphysical truth, you become aware of the reality of your being and of life itself. This follows naturally through an awareness of consciousness of God and your relationship to Him. When the awakening starts to dawn upon you, it opens the door to a whole new world. Your new being sees that negativity has no place whatever in this newfound existence, because you become aware of the perfection of God's creation and you are no longer in the quicksand of false theories, screaming headlines of economic disaster, psychic predictions of great calamities, and an unwarranted fear of the future. You can look at all of these things with a new vision and behold the beauty of Angels dwelling among you, ready and willing at all times to aid and help you in every way.

In order to have the right awareness, you must be alert at all times. Watch your thinking and your actions with diligence, because the "little foxes can spoil the vines." Those little foxes can be moments of impatience, intolerance of others, gossip and lack of gratitude, which is one of the greatest sins of omission you can commit. The vines are the spiritual roots that have begun to grow. They are tender and easily destroyed, until they have gone deep, deep into your consciousness and are strong enough to withstand any storm of outward affairs. Until then they have to be cared for with gentleness and watered with great love and protection. These vines are jewels, precious and rare, and must be guarded well. The strength and the depth of their growth indicates how deeply you have realized your real spiritual selves. Your consciousness has to be lifted very high to make you aware of Angels and to understand the major part they play in your lives.

I would like to relate a beautiful demonstration of how these heavenly Angels operate when you call upon them properly. Juana, my precious friend and housekeeper, lost her purse. It slipped out of the car and onto the street when her car door, which had been slightly sprung, opened. Juana reached over and closed it, and she didn't notice the absence of her purse as she was holding her sister's baby. When they got out of the car to go into a store to shop, she realized her purse was missing and that it had fallen out. She drove back over the street where she thought it might be— but no purse. She inquired around at several places nearby, without any success. In her purse was her rent money in cash, checks for her utilities, her checkbook, her driver's license, and some valuable jewelry given to her by her mother. Juana of course reported this to the police. Then she called me. I assured her that the purse would be returned. She said, "Oh yes, I'm praying—so is my son."

That evening about six o'clock, she called me again and said a man had called her and had found her purse on the street. This was a Friday. He said he would return it Monday morning. Juana asked about the money and the jewelry, and the man said that there was nothing in the purse but her wallet and some papers. When she told me this I immediately went to work with the Angels. I asked for a visualization of the man who found the purse. I saw him distinctly. Then I surrounded him with Angels and declared out loud that he could not use the money or dispose of the jewelry in any way.

The next morning when Juana came I described the man to her, what he would be wearing and even to the fact that he had a mustache and that he would bring her purse back complete. Monday morning, he came to her door with a friend and gave her back the purse with everything intact. He even refused a reward. Juana said that he was the one I saw and described to her, even to the blue jeans he was wearing.

This shows you how powerful this Angelic study can be. Of course, Juana's faith is absolutely unwavering. Her heart is pure. Therefore, she is a marvelous instrument for the Truth to work through. Her conscious awareness accepts without equivocation the Allness of God and the Power of the Angels.

Here is what some of our great Masters and Teachers have said about consciousness:

Yogananda, founder of Self-Realization Fellowship, says, "To know God, you must experience Him within your own consciousness. Rise above an ordinary life into a higher realm of consciousness."

Mary Baker Eddy, discoverer and founder of Christian Science, states, "Consciousness constructs a better body when faith in matter has been conquered. Correct material belief by spiritual understanding and spirit will form you anew."

Joel Goldsmith, founder of the infinite Way, says, "If you have a consciousness of God as supply and a consciousness of God as the source of all beauty, intelligence, wisdom, and guidance and protection, that is all you will ever need."

These great leaders and teachers realized so completely that everything that God created is ever at hand, because it all lies within our consciousness of our complete and absolute oneness with God and the Angels. The treasure is all there, "Closer than breathing and nearer than hands and feet."

"I and My Father are one," said Jesus. "I am one with all, my health, my joy, my prosperity, my companionship." Repeat this and let it live within you until your consciousness becomes so aware that manifestations can come instantly.

Your consciousness is *you*, the real *you*. Some of us show different faces to different people, but underneath is the real us. Keep it beautiful and on a high plane. Most faces reveal the thinking within. And if you are constantly being aware of your God-consciousness, your outward appearance will reveal this at once.

Don't live in the past. Yesterday has gone forever. Unless it has been a lovely experience, you should never discuss it, and should train yourself to forget it. Now is the only time. Make each moment a beautiful now. You are the master of your life. If circumstances seem to arise that seem difficult, turn irrevocably to God and the Angels.

These untoward things arise to make you prove what your real consciousness is. When the results of your prayers become evident, then you know that you are on the right path. Stay there! Don't allow your consciousness to be diverted into many different channels. This cannot be stressed too much. The Law of Truth is absolute and final. If you have seen and witnessed the results, then do not deviate. Remember, one of the greatest tests is the peace you feel within your heart. There is a beautiful hymn that I sing called "The Lord Has Given Me a Song." He has given every one of you a song. And if your heart sings it, you know that you are really dwelling in God-awareness and God-consciousness, for Angels dwell in harmony and the beauty of a song brings it out—loud, or within your heart.

The Bible states, "Have the Mind in you which was also in Christ Jesus." Having that mind is having the consciousness of Light and Love and living it.

Consciousness is like a flower. Its petals uncurl to the light of understanding. Nurture it with unselfishness and make the soil around it rich with *love, compassion,* and *forgiveness.* Then your full–blown flower will bloom radiant in the sunshine of God's great beneficence, and the power of the Angels' devotion to mankind.

Chapter Ten
Healings (Letters)

This healing took place some time ago, but the results surrounding it are certainly worth telling you.

My son was a young man at the time and he had a pal by the name of Robert who attended his school. One day Robert met Ron with tears in his eyes. Ronnie became concerned because Robert was always such a happy-go-lucky kid, so he asked him what the problem was.

"Is it a girl or something?" queried Ron.

"No, no, nothing like that," answered Robert. "It's my mother; she's terribly sick, and no practitioner has been able to help her."

"Well that's easy, Robert, just send her to my mom and she'll be healed."

The next day Irene, Robert's mother, came to see me. She told me that she had had an issue of blood for over a year and was afraid to go to a doctor because of the world belief about such a condition. Irene had been a student of Christian Science for many years.

I asked her if she knew the meaning of the word "blood" and she said she did not, and had never really thought about it as having a meaning.

"Blood stands for Life," I said. "And since we know that God gave you life, and sustains it, then we understand what the word means. So, Irene, you can't lose anything that stands for God, can you?"

Irene pondered this for a moment, then she said, "No, I guess you are right."

She left feeling better and when she called me the next day she was completely healed. So much so that she asked me to help her to find a job. She visited me again and we talked about her right place in the Kingdom of God.

"You see, Poleete," she said to me, "I'm over forty and jobs are not growing on trees for a woman my age."

"Nonsense," I rejoined. "There is no age or time in God's Kingdom—God never made a clock or a calendar—man did that humanly, and thus his problems."

"Yes, I realize that. In *Science and Health* by Mary Baker Eddy, she says, 'never record ages; chronological data is no part of man'," replied Irene. "But I never quite understood how you would go about doing this."

"Simple," was my reply. "Just take the limitations off of yourself and realize your complete oneness with your creator—God. You are humanly aware of your years, God isn't."

"How do I do that?" asked Irene.

"By getting in tune with the Great Beings of Light and the Angels, whom God created for you," was my answer.

"I guess I haven't thought much about Angels," said Irene.

"Well, my dear, read your Bible and references on Angels by Mrs. Eddy. You'll be surprised what you will learn," I answered. "But now let us think of the word 'place' for you. Jesus said, 'I go to prepare a place for you!' So of course, your job is already waiting for you, Irene—and a good one."

"I hope so. I've been out of work for too long," said Irene, "but now I will do as you suggested and try to take off my own thoughts of limitation."

The following week Irene called me and said to her great astonishment she had two offers of jobs. And the second place didn't ask her to fill out an age application—only her work qualifications. This was a secretarial job at Harris and Frank, which she took, and she stayed there for about five years until another great event took place in her life (which I will tell you about after this occurrence) which had all the earmarks of a miracle.

Irene came over one Saturday and started the conversation thusly:

"Poleete, since such wonderful things have taken place in my life, I was wondering if you could take up another problem for us that has been hanging over our heads—my two daughters and my son—for two years now?"

"Describe what it is all about, Irene. There's always an answer to every problem," was my reply.

"Well," continued Irene, "two years ago my mother-in-law passed away and left a will that is so involved that no attorney will handle it. You see, after her son, my husband, passed on, I married again and she was very angry at me for doing so and wrote her will in such a way that would assure her that me and my son by my new husband would not be beneficiaries in any way—only the two girls, who were her son's children."

I pondered this for a while before I spoke. Then suggested, "Why don't we look up the word inheritance in our Bibles and in the dictionary. After all, you know in the Bible it states, 'Ye are heirs to the Kingdom of God!'"

Irene agreed to do her part. One week later to the day, her eldest daughter, who lived back east, called her, saying, "Mother, I've found a fine attorney who will take our case with Grandma's will for a small fee, so we are ready to go."

One month later, Irene's younger daughter received her share of the estate, which included a car, some property, and $20,000. Irene's precious daughter Diane wanted to share with her mother, so she bought them all a lovely home in the Valley where I was invited to dinner so we could all rejoice and express gratitude for the goodness of God.

But it didn't end there; this saga of Irene goes on. One day Irene came to see me. "Poleete," she began, "I'm really lonely. My daughter has her friends and is gone a great deal and so is my son, who is now a teenager."

"You are saying that you would like to have a husband," was my answer.

"Yes, if I could meet the right one this time. My divorce has been final now for several years. I've met several men since, but no one has been Mr. Right," was Irene's reply.

"Irene, then we had better get busy and find you a husband. The Angels are always finding things, so I guess this shouldn't be too difficult." We both laughed.

"How do we go about this?" asked Irene.

"First, let us think what the word 'husband' means," I answered. "It means 'taking care of.' A husbandman, for instance, who plants flowers, cares for them—thus the meaning of the word."

"It would be great to have someone to take care of me," smiled Irene. "I've been on my own for a long time. My first husband was a fine man, but he passed on when my two girls were two and four. Then my second husband was a drinker and a waster. Our marriage was short-lived."

"Let us not look back, Irene," I said. "Yesterday is gone and we can't and should not relive it, even in memory, except the good and wonderful parts—and those only momentarily. There are too many beautiful things awaiting us if we walk on the marvelous path that God created for each of us."

"I believe you—really I sincerely do, Poleete. I have witnessed so many blessings I can't complain," said Irene. "Am I wrong in wanting a companion?"

"Indeed not. It is natural for a woman to want a husband, just as it is for a man to want a wife. A good marriage is a lovely part of life. The twenty-third Psalm comes to my mind. 'The Lord is my shepherd, I shall not want,' the opening line. Let us think about that for a moment. We know that the Lord is our shepherd, so He has already filled our wants, hasn't He? And in it states, 'The Lord is thy husband,' so there you have it. Stay with those statements from the Bible. Also know that you cannot lack one iota of good in your life because there are no vacancies. I'll be with you." Irene left very encouraged and with a happy smile on her beautiful face.

Two months passed and Irene and her daughter Diane planned to spend their vacations together. They decided to visit a cousin in Sacramento, whom they hadn't seen for many years, and who had constantly invited them to spend some time with her and her family. The first evening they were there, Irene's cousin Marion asked Irene if she would mind if she invited a widower who was employed by the city, for dinner.

"He is a fine man," said Marion. "He doesn't smoke or drink. His wife passed away two years ago and I told him about you, so he is eager to meet you. His first name is Byron."

Irene told me later that it was "love at first sight." Byron proposed to her the second week of her vacation. She called me and told me about the whirlwind romance. Irene returned to the Valley to sell her home as she planned to marry Byron and move to Sacramento. Byron was willing to have her daughter and son live with them. He had a large home with a swimming pool and lovely grounds. He seemed, Irene said, to be happy to have a family living in the house again. He had a son who was away at college studying to be a doctor, so he was living alone with the exception of a housekeeper.

Irene asked for help in selling her house, so it was sold in a matter of weeks. She left for Sacramento and, of course, married Byron. But that isn't the end of the story. Her daughter Diane, when she met Byron's son, fell in love with him, and they were also married a few months after Irene and Byron. I heard from Irene for some time after this, and "all was well."

You see, Irene had complete confidence, and that is what it takes, along with the right kind of study. I gave her everything I could to aid her understanding, and she was a very apt student. The precious Angels made themselves felt in this beautiful healing of Irene.

An Actor Speaks
by Basil Hoffman

When I was in my twenties, I began to develop a physical condition which made it difficult to grasp a pen between my forefinger and thumb of my right hand, making writing clumsy and painful. Over the next few years the manifestation of the condition intensified, and it became impossible to write more than a word or two without experiencing great pain, while at the same time my entire hand would begin to curl inward so that I could not even hold the pen and paper.

There was probably some idea of heredity in this as well, because my mother, grandfather and two aunts experienced problems with their right (writing) hands. Those problems ranged from tremors to the inability to hold a writing instrument. The adjustment I finally made was to begin to write left-handed, which I did quite successfully. However, the affliction in my right hand continued to make its presence known periodically in the form of a slight tremor when I was tired or anxious, and a cramping when I held a key in a lock if any extraordinary pressure was required.

I finally consulted a renowned neurologist and orthopedic surgeon who had some previous knowledge of my condition, which he called "focal action dyatona." Even with his great experience and expertise, all his attempts to alleviate the symptoms, even with expensive medication, were totally unsuccessful. At this point I abandoned all interest in dealing with the problem ever again, particularly since my left-hand writing was more than satisfactory and any other inconveniences were minimal. But my wife, Christine, was not satisfied that I had solved the problem by making an adjustment to it. She wanted me to accept nothing less than a complete healing of the condition and, to that end, strongly urged me to get help from her spiritual teacher and healer, Poleete Carabel. Although I had met Poleete socially and liked her, being an atheist I had no interest in her spiritual work, healing or otherwise.

My dear wife Christine insisted upon my attending Poleete's Angel class. I balked for a while, but I did go and to my surprise, I enjoyed it. Then I decided to follow my wife's insistence and visit the Reverend Poleete privately. This was really the beginning of my new life. I went to Poleete for a treatment. Poleete treated my hand spiritually, silently, and with no physical manipulation or technique that I could see. After the treatment, Poleete asked me to write something, and I did, with no discomfort. My right hand had been healed in about twenty minutes.

The experience changed my life dramatically, because it ultimately led to my being healed of atheism. A whole new universe of spiritual concepts had been opened up to me, for which I am eternally grateful.

Basil Hoffman

Healings

These healings have all come to me in letters, so they can be verified as I told you before.

Dearest Poleete,

I find it very difficult to put my gratitude on paper for all the blessings you have bestowed on me, the healings, the invaluable teachings, and enlightenment—but I will try.

In May of 1987, I awoke with tremendous pain in my left breast. It was hard to my touch and inflamed with intense heat. Because of my studies and new knowledge, which I found with you, Poleete, my panic was short lived. I knew what collective thought would name it, and I decided that *this* was going to be handled spiritually. I refused to accept the verdict of **materia medica** and called you, Poleete, for help in healing. I told no one else as negative fears, I knew, would be damaging. I could not even stand to have a sheet over me at night. You gave me my first treatment and the pain was greatly reduced. You continued to work for me every day. I saw you one more time the following week. By the end of two weeks I was completely healed, with not a trace of the problem.

God bless you, Poleete. All my love.
Sandi Wirth

> *(Sandi is a famous animal trainer who lives in the San Fernando Valley.)*

This next case was indeed amazing in every aspect. I will quote just part of his letter—but the part I do use is authentic, and can be authenticated whenever one wishes to do so.

Mental Illness Healed

This particular case came to me some time ago. I have witnessed healings many times of what the *materia medica* said were severe cases, but this one stands out in my memory because of the complexity of the situation.

I was getting prepared for a singing engagement for a banquet to be given by the Hollywood American Legion. I had my own accompanist, but the Legion wanted me to use their pianist. She was a young woman by the name of Mary. We talked on the phone and made an appointment in my home for a rehearsal. She played well, but I noticed a very sad expression across her face. So, I finally asked her what was troubling her so much. The tears started streaming down her face as she related her story.

"My twenty-one-year-old son," she began, "is incarcerated in a mental institution, and the doctors contacted me last week stating that perhaps an operation on his brain would cure his condition. But they told me in honesty that he had only a fifty-fifty chance for survival, that it could prove fatal. I am the one who has to make the decision, and I don't know what to do."

My heart went out to this mother. I asked her if she believed in spiritual healing. Her answer was "yes" but she didn't really understand it. She said that when her son was a small child, a neighbor suggested a healer to her during a time when the boy was desperately ill with measles, and that he had been miraculously cured in one day.

"Do you know anyone who does healing?" she asked me hopefully. "Do you?"

"Yes, I am in the healing work," I answered.

"Will you take my son's case?" was her instant query. I agreed to pray for Ralph.

I immediately sat down and wrote to some church people in the vicinity who gave out religious literature. I thought the contact would benefit Ralph. Then I wrote directly to him, giving him some spiritual direction and letting the young man know that we were with him in prayer.

One month later, Mary, his mother, called me and said the doctors in the sanitarium had contacted her to say that Ralph was entirely healed, had passed all the tests and was ready to be released. The operation never took place, only the operation of God's truth. Ralph was seated in my living room looking very handsome and well just a week after his recovery. He and his mother opened up a novelty store in a little town near San Diego and became very successful. I heard from them frequently and all was well.

These beautiful experiences prove constantly the power of the Angels if we but use it correctly and give these shining Beings our complete love and faith.

June 20, 1987
Poleete,

I wanted to write and let you know how much your support and healings have meant to me and my son. I was skeptical about healings prior to working with you because of the so-called "ministers" I have seen on T.V. who supposedly do healings by yelling, screaming, or whatever other means of hysterics. However, you have always been quiet, clear, and worked so wonderfully with us.

I brought my son to you in the summer of 1986 because he had been on Tegretal since he was 7 years old for seizure activity. I was always uncomfortable with him taking the medicine because of long–term side effects; however, when he would forget to take his medicine or the dosage was too low based on his growing weight, the seizures would start again. He was 14 when I brought him to you for a healing, and I can say since that time he has not had another seizure nor has he taken any seizure medicine. In addition, I have had to call on you several times when anxiety attacks or heart palpitations started. Over the phone, instantly, I received a healing, and I am so grateful for your help, support, and belief in me. Thank you so much.

Love,
Theresa

An Alcoholic and a Drug User Finds God

This letter came to me from a young woman who felt her life was a terrible mess and was hopeless. She asked for a "reading," and after I gave her one, she stayed and talked about her situation. I of course told her there was no such thing as a hopeless condition, because God created all good, and so anything anywhere can be healed if we only believed enough in the power of Angels (and, of course, God who created them for us). After several sessions with me she sent me this letter. (She had also attended my Angel class.)

Dear Poleete (for your readers),

I was at the end of my rope and didn't know which way to turn! For fifteen years, beer and pills were the largest part of my husband's life. And if that wasn't enough, he added cocaine and whiskey also. He definitely was not the man I married. He was arrested for drunk driving, put in jail for five days, and ordered to go to an alcoholic school for one year by the courts. But it didn't take any effect whatsoever.

I went to some of the meetings with him, to support him in any way I could. But Burt, my husband, always said he wasn't like those people. He would not ever admit he had a problem.

I saw a counselor for advice on what I should do. I didn't know which way to turn. She said, "You've got two choices...you leave him, or you learn to live with it. If you choose to live with it, you have to learn to live your own separate life." I chose to try living with him. For the next five years I buried myself in my work, fortunately work I loved and believed in. Animals were my other love. I was successful in a pet grooming business, and spent many hours working with animals in the movie and television industry. One of my goals was human casting and working with other trainers.

One day I met another trainer. We became friends and about a year later when I felt lost and lonely, we talked on the phone. Sandi (the trainer) told me about a lovely lady by the name of Poleete who helped her with her animals and through a particularly rough time in her life.

I called Poleete for an appointment, at which time she gave me a "reading." I have to admit I was very skeptical. She told me that Burt would die shortly if he didn't stop the dope and drinking. I believed her because I saw him deteriorate before my eyes from 200 to 145 pounds. I was also terrified that he was going to kill me, because he went into such terrible rages and didn't seem to know what he was doing at the time. But Poleete said when I told her this, "No, Kim, I see great success for your future personally and no one is going to kill you. Rest assured of this fact." I left her house feeling better than I had in a very long time.

Having been raised a staunch Catholic, I was wary as I had been warned never to go beyond the Church. But since I felt I was losing my mind, Poleete was my last resort.

I was invited to one of Poleete's Angel classes with Sandi. On the walls of Poleete's were pictures of Christ and lots of Angel figures. I suddenly felt at peace and that it was all right for me to be there.

The information I learned at the Angel class I put to use and it worked! That class turned me around. I stopped worrying so much about myself, and began working on ways to help other people.

I went back to Poleete for a second "reading." She saw Burt going away. I told Poleete that I would like to bring him to her but I couldn't even get him to go to the corner store. She said, "Kim, you and I have to get busy now and help him." She spiritualized his name and instructed me to read it to him.

I said, "But he'll be drunk."

She answered, "Do it anyway, and read the 91st Psalm at least three times a day, using his name in it."

That night I picked him up at a bar at midnight—completely drunk. He was absolutely incoherent but nevertheless I told him I had something very nice for him. When we arrived home, I read him the spiritualization of his name. He was very quiet and he really listened, in spite of being so drunk. Surprisingly, he asked me to read it again. I did, and he began to cry and said, "Am I really getting to be that bad?"

I replied, "I have turned it over to God. I myself can no longer help you!"

That second "reading" I had with Poleete took place on a Thursday in the fall of 1987. One week later, to the day, my husband committed himself to Studio 12, a recovery house for drug and alcohol abuse. This miracle happened after twenty years of his denying he had a problem!

Today he is now house manager and a counselor of Studio 12, helping others get rid of the habit.

Thank you, Poleete. Every day of my life now is like a new beginning. You have been my guiding Angel.
Kim Lindenoen

This next letter was a surprise to me. I knew, of course, that this young woman had had a healing, but I was unaware of the entire problem until I received this letter a few days ago:

Dear Poleete,
This note is to thank you with all my heart for your love and prayers in helping me through a medical problem.

In the summer of 1984, I found, much to my dismay, that I had an illness that in many cases was incurable. This I never believed because I had read a book by Joel Goldsmith that brings out the reality of good and the unreality of anything unlike God. However, due to the circumstances surrounding me (being that I was not of legal age and my parents insisted that I be given radiation treatments as the doctor suggested) I went through a year of radiation treatments, going two to three times a week. Then I had to take another test to see the results of the radiation treatments, which proved to have no effect whatsoever. The problem was still there, worse than before. So the next suggestion was that I take chemotherapy treatments immediately. All this time I refused to read any of the pamphlets on the so-called "disease" because I refused to make it that real. I made up my mind not to take the chemotherapy after my sister told me about you. I called and made an appointment to see you. My healing started at once. But it took several weeks to clear my thinking completely. So along with your treatments, which were completely spiritual, I also started studying with you. Thanks to your works and prayers, I did not have to go through the horror of chemotherapy. I was healed! Three years have passed and I feel great and grateful!
Love you,
F.

This young woman fully realized that I was only an instrument through which her healing came—God and His Angels gave us the knowledge and the privilege of doing this and seeing a radiant, smiling young person instead of a sad, frightened one.

These are just a few of the healings that I have had the great pleasure of witnessing in my very happy, marvelous life. Anyone who is willing to "fast" from worldly things and be dedicated, can witness the same results. Jesus said, "Greater works than these shall ye do." He also said, "Ye are the light of the world"—and so you are made up of light—each and every one of you.

Chapter Eleven
The Healings of Animals

I have witnessed many, many healings with animals, and I will relate some of them. This one was "close to home" as they say. It happened to be my niece Jean's dog.

One day Jean called me and said that she and her husband had just taken their dog, Shamrock, to the vet. The veterinarian had said that Shamrock had a fatal condition and that there was nothing they could do for him. So as a last resort, I was called.

I asked her to bring Shamrock over, which she did. Shamrock isn't Irish, but he is very precious and quite witty in his own way. I spiritualized his name before Jean came. After she was here, I talked silently to Shamrock's Angels (oh yes, all animals have Angels; so do plants). His Angels were very cooperative, as are all Angels. I held him in my arms and told him about his absolute perfection. He listened patiently. Jean and I sat talking and suddenly Shamrock was missing. When he had come into the house he had scarcely been able to walk. We looked around in the kitchen and upstairs, but no Shamrock. Pretty soon he came bounding up the stairs.

"He's been investigating the house," I said.

"But look, Auntie, how spry he is. He is healed," said my niece, looking happy but surprised.

"Of course," was my reply.

After Jean left, I had occasion to use the downstairs bathroom, and there on the floor by the toilet were nine hard lumps about the size of golf balls. Shamrock had passed them. I called Jean and told her. She was amazed because she said the vet had told her that those "things" were in him. She also added that Shamrock, in the seven years they had him, had never, never used the carpet or any part of the house for his eliminations. He was thoroughly housebroken. It was just as though he wanted us to know what had happened. Which I am certain was the case. This was two years ago, and he is still well and sassy.

My voice teacher's cat Pancho also had a marvelous healing. Nellie called me and said that Pancho was very sick.

"I'll be right over," was my reply. Nellie lived a short distance from my house, about five miles or so. When I arrived, Nellie met me on the porch crying and said Pancho had just passed away.

"Put him on your bed and leave me alone with him," I said confidently.

I talked to Pancho and his Angels. I spent about forty-five minutes with him. At the end of that time, he jumped off the bed and was completely healed. Nellie was almost in a state of shock when she saw him walking out of the room.

"But...but," she stammered, "I know he was gone. I felt his heart and it had stopped."

"It's going now," I said with a laugh.

After that Pancho, who had always so disliked hearing people sing that he would hide during Nellie's lessons, came every time I was there and stood on top of the piano, purring and thanking me, much to Nellie's astonishment, because he came out for no one else. He knew what had taken place. And they call animals dumb!

This is a healing that I must tell because the circumstances surrounding it were unusual:

One day I was "reading" for a young man, and during the course of conversation he told me that he had a little dog whose back legs had become useless. I asked him to bring the dog to me, that she could be healed.

"Oh, I don't believe in anything like spiritual healings or even in God," was his answer, "but I will bring her over anyway."

My statement was, "Well, your dog will know and understand. Animals are easily healed because they are so intuitive. It doesn't matter that you don't believe—I do and your dog does."

About a week later, the young man brought Heidie to see me. I took her in my arms. She looked at me and we communicated instantly. The next day she was healed, and now is running as well as she ever did.

To say that the young man was astonished is putting it mildly. He said that the vet who had been attending her could hardly believe what his eyes saw.

Angels are around animals, very special ones. It just takes someone to recognize them and they do the rest.

I have witnessed many, many healings of animals throughout my ministry. One outstanding one was with a neighbor's cat, Jimmie. He used to pay daily calls on us. I noticed that at times he limped badly and also he would seem to have trouble breathing correctly. His owner told me that he had arthritis in one leg and asthma. While she was telling me this, I was silently affirming that there were no such things or words in the Kingdom of God. The next time Jimmie came for a visit, I held him in my arms and told him this. He listened intently and was instantaneously healed. He was supposed to be well along in years, too.

Later a lump developed on his back but the Angels soon took care of that and Jimmie lived a long healthy life—free from all these claims of error that did not belong to him.

Another demonstration of the power of Angels was for a bird. A lady called me in great distress, and said that her parakeet was lost. She allowed Tweety (his name) to fly around the room for a while every day and she accidentally left a window open and out flew Tweety. He had never been outside before and had been missing for three days when she called me. She had left the window open in hopes that he would find his way home.

"I'm so worried about him," she cried, "because a horrid cat could get him and he also wouldn't know how to find food or water."

"Don't worry," I said, "we will have the Angels find your Tweety and send him back. Put his cage in the open window and trust."

She called me the next day, overjoyed. Sure enough, her little bird did come back. He went right into his cage and ate and drank, talking all the time, she said, about his adventure. (She understood his bird-talk.)

Another animal healing had to do with a horse who was a greatly loved pet by the entire family. The master, who lived in Big Bear, called me about ten o'clock one night and said that Jerry, the horse, was dying. The vet was there in attendance and had done all he knew to do. I assured the family that Jerry would be all right and that we would attend to it at once. I worked on the absolute perfection of all of God's ideas, which certainly included Jerry. He had not eaten for several days and just lay quietly on his side; now and then he appeared to be in pain.

About an hour after Jerry's master called, he got up, looked around, and started eating. He was galloping the next day, and lived to a ripe age.

These memories are very happy ones for me. I don't need to have the greatness and majesty of God proven to me, but I rejoice each time something lovely takes place, because I realize that it shows others what can be done—if we Love God enough and use Angel Power.

I think this is a good time to mention another healing that the owner of a dog sent to me. I am using her exact words as she wrote it:

Dearest Poleete:

Every time I look at my big beautiful Golden Retriever, Reggie, I give thanks to God for his miraculous healing which took place through you. His story has been an inspiration to many and I hope through being told through your book, many more will be inspired to seek a spiritual solution to any problem.

My husband (to whom I was married at that time) is a prominent attorney, and I was preparing food for a party. We left our back door open so that our six-month-old puppy, Reggie, could wander in and out. All of a sudden we noticed he was limping and seemed to be in pain. I immediately rushed him to the veterinarian. They had me leave him for X-rays, and I was to check back later that day. When I did so, they suggested that I confer with an orthopedic veterinarian specialist who was on the staff there. Apparently Reggie had fallen and had severely damaged the cartilage in his shoulder and leg.

We were told that he would have to have an operation, or be in pain the rest of his life. The worst news was yet to come; they would cut away the damaged cartilage, they said, and a fibroid cartilage would form. This is not as elastic as a regular cartilage, they further explained, and he would be left with a permanent limp.

There were other complications. For a reason unknown, the damage would spread to the opposite shoulder within a two or three year period, and a second operation would be necessary, thus leaving the dog a virtual cripple for the rest of his life.

We couldn't believe it. I took him to two more specialists and was given the same answer each time. Then I sat in my car bewildered, and asking God for an answer. Your name flashed before me. I called you and asked if you worked for animals. I'll never forget your answer, which was, "Of course, my dear, they have their Angels the same as you and I."

It was a divine inspiration as Reggie received a beautiful, complete healing and is the perfect creature that God intended him to be.

My other four animals, since then, have had wonderful healings of many different ailments—all with the same marvelous results.

I am eternally grateful to you, Poleete, for your complete dedication.

Sincerely,
Christine Fadel

Chapter Twelve
Predictions
A Happy Ending

One day I was "reading" for a young woman who, at the time, was fashion coordinator for a large downtown department store. She was a lovely looking girl; well groomed, in fashionable attire, and had above average good looks.

As I was "reading," I was surprised to see that she was not dating anyone. I mentioned this and she said, "Oh, I've given up. I just can't seem to meet anyone suitable."

"But you will," I assured her, "and you will get married, leave this country, and have a child."

She laughed at this and her reply came fast. "That is all impossible. To begin with, I don't know anyone marriageable, I'm almost forty, so I won't have any children ever, and in view of the fact that I have a fine position at an excellent salary, I can't see myself leaving the job or the country."

"However, Madelaine, you will do all of these things that you are so certain will never be," I insisted.

"Some things that you have told me I can believe, but not that," was her rejoinder.

I didn't hear a word from Madelaine for almost a year. One day she called and asked if she might come for another "reading." I set up an appointment for her and over she came, looking positively radiant.

"Well, Poleete, you hit everything on the nose. The man you described came into my life in a very unusual way, as you said he would. I was giving a lecture on fashions and this man was seated in the front row. After the lecture he came up to me, introduced himself as a manufacturer of clothing from Germany, and invited me to dinner that evening. I went. We fell deeply in love. I quit my good position, left for Germany with him, and we were married there after I had met his family. So I am visiting here now and I came especially for a 'reading' all the way from Germany. Now what do you see?"

"The first thing," I smiled, "is that you are pregnant. You may not know it yet—but you are, and it's a boy."

"Yes, I do know, and my husband wants a boy very much. This time I will believe you. I should, after the amazing things that have happened to me. My entire life has changed."

I heard from Madelaine seven months later, and it was a boy!

Holy Matrimony

One evening I was present at a wedding that I had predicted. It was telecast over Station 40 in Santa Ana, California.

Marianne, the bride, became engaged to Scotty while she was in the Holy Land. It was evidently a whirlwind romance. I had predicted the marriage and the trip to Marianne during a reading some time ago. She felt that she might be married someday again, but said, "Now Poleete, where would I ever get the money to go on a trip across the ocean?" I declared that she would, and of course she did.

It was beautiful to see Marianne married in such lovely surroundings. Channel 40 is used for religious purposes only. It was the first wedding to be performed over this station. Channel 40 is doing wonderful work for people all over the country. Calls for healing work pour in constantly and letters are read from those who have received instantaneous help.

My heart rejoices to know that so many, many people who were non-believers, are now seeking spiritual healings. This is proof to me of what I have seen for a long time—an upsurge toward God and the Angels. Marianne's marriage in this holy atmosphere is bound to be a lasting and joyous one.

A Baby Arrives at Last

Ethel came for a "reading" while she was visiting here from the east coast. I saw a baby being born to her oldest daughter. Ethel laughed at this and said, "Of all the impossible things I can think of, that would be it. My daughter has been married for fifteen years. They have tried in every way to have a child, but with no success. So we have all given up."

"Then you will be pleasantly surprised, because a lovely, healthy baby is going to be conceived by your daughter before the year is out."

I then saw a very unhappy problem connected with Ethel's son.

"Yes," said Ethel with tears in her eyes, "he has a serious drinking problem."

"He will stop drinking," I said confidently," but Ethel, you must help him."

"How?" she asked. "I'll do anything I can."

"By using the 91st Psalm for him at least twice a day. A mother's prayers, filled with great love, are very powerful. I know that your boy will receive the healing he needs." I was positive about this.

I didn't hear from Ethel for a whole year until the other day. Her daughter had a "reading" party in her home and her mother was visiting again and waiting eagerly for a "reading" and a chance to tell me the good news.

"Well, Poleete, a few months after I was here, my other daughter did become pregnant, and now has a fine baby. I did as you suggested and used the 91st Psalm daily for my son. He stopped drinking entirely and he now has a good job and a happy family. I am so grateful." Tears filled Ethel's eyes as she told me; tears of gladness.

Chapter 13
Business and How to Succeed

Jesus said to his mother when she found him in the temple teaching, "Knowest ye not that I must be about my Father's business?" He had been gone for three days and his mother was naturally concerned, but his answer told her that he was starting on the career that later took him into teaching and healing.

You cannot all be teachers and healers, because the world in which we dwell has to have different forms of activity. But one of your endeavors can definitely be "your Father's business," and if you think of it as such, then it has to be joyous and successful. Never feel that any task that is honest work is menial. Lift up whatever you are doing to a high sense of consciousness.

I remember when I learned this, at a very tender age. My young husband John had passed away, leaving me with a baby to support. John had always earned good money. We had a nice home, a car, and a live-in housekeeper. The furniture was paid for, but the car was not. So when he died, the car went back to the finance company. I had never worked in my life except in my own home, but I did have a good education. I had attended college after my marriage, so I thought that getting a job would be simple. However, when I took stock of what I could do, I suddenly realized that my education had all been along literary lines, with nothing very practical to make a living. (Although later on this changed and the literary training became invaluable.) So I proceeded to try and find employment.

Everywhere I went the same question was asked, "What experience have you had?" My answer always had to be "None." One day when discouragement almost overwhelmed me, I passed a building downtown and noticed a sign for the Green Employment Agency. I was plenty green about everything, so I ventured in. The man who ran it was very nice. He too asked me what I could do, and I stammered out, "Nothing, I guess."

He looked at me compassionately and asked if I had ever worked in a cafeteria? My answer of course was "No."

"Well," he said, "I do have an opening in a cafeteria in Vernon, but you will have to say you have had experience."

"I don't even know where Vernon is, and besides, I can't tell a lie," was my sad rejoinder.

"I'll tell you what I will do," he said. "I'll call them and I am sending you and I will tell them you are experienced. Okay?"

I muttered something. At this point I was not only at my rope's end after two weeks of pounding the pavement, but I was also tired. So I agreed to go to Vernon. Mr. Green gave me the address and directions. I had to take two streetcars and a bus to get there. It was four in the afternoon when I arrived, and the sky was gray and sunless, and so was I.

When I entered the cafeteria it was like a great barn, clean but dismal. A greasy-looking cook met me with, "So you are the one Mr. Green sent. Pretty young, aren't you?"

"Oh, I even have a baby," was my quick reply as I stretched myself up to my full five feet. (I grew an inch more later on.)

"Well, we will try you out," said the cook rather reluctantly. "Be here at seven tomorrow morning."

I had to arise at five to be at the cafeteria at seven. It was a long way from Hollywood, where I lived. I had never gotten up so early in my life, but I was happy to have a job. The sad part was leaving my baby. The picture I took with me was seeing him screaming in the arms of my good friend who came to take care of him.

My first few days at the cafeteria were memorable, believe me. The first day the cook asked me to cut the bread for sandwiches. He handed me a knife that was almost as long as I was. I started cutting real good until the middle of the long loaf, then somehow the knife went sideways and the slices got larger and larger. The cook came by and saw it. He took the knife from me and finished himself. "Can you cut pies?" he asked.

I looked at the big pies hesitantly, so he said, "Here, I'll show you how." I learned that even cutting pies took a certain technique, which I certainly didn't have. Then he asked me if I knew how to make coffee, and I answered with a bold, "Oh, yes"—until he brought me into the dining area and showed me a big urn way above my head. He looked at me again and saw the tragic "I don't know how" expression on my face, so he showed me the way to make coffee for at least a hundred people. I had to stand on a stool, lift up a heavy pail of boiling water, and pour it over the coffee grounds.

In a week I became an adept coffee maker, a great pie–cutter, an expert 100-pounds of ice–chipper, a fast salt–and–pepper–and–mustard– and–catsup–filler. My first duty in the early morning hours was to scrub the tables. At first this was difficult, but I sang all the songs I knew while I worked. No one was there but the dishwasher and the cook. The dishwasher told me later that he enjoyed the singing, that it made his work easier. He was a strange person. He had been a Canadian Mountie and had gotten into some kind of trouble. He washed dishes in two different restaurants in order to keep his son in military school. He said he hadn't learned anything else to do.

When my mother heard that I was working in what she called a "lowly job," she cried. I explained to her that I was happy because I was busy. She only said, "With your looks, your talent, your intelligence—all wasted." She was a mother, and all mothers, I guess, think their children are geniuses (or almost). But I knew that God and the Angels would place me in a better position. This was a valuable learning period. I had to see the other side of the working world, not only to appreciate what was later in store for me, but to be able to help other people and to understand better what life was all about.

Each morning, as I rode the streetcars and busses, I would pray silently, and with each turn of the wheels beneath me repeat, "God, I know You will have something better for me, but I will be grateful now for what I am doing," and I was.

Three months later I received a phone call from a man I knew. He said, "There's an opening for an editor on a newspaper and your name kept coming to me."

My first thought was to say "No, I can't ever do that—but instead I said, "When can I start?" with more boldness in my voice than I felt at the moment, believe me. (My first book *Poleete* tells in detail of my many experiences as editor of the paper, and how God and the Angels directed my every move.)

In both instances I was "On my Father's business." The first *seemed* lowly—there actually is no lowly task, if we are serving others. However, I lifted it up and went to the top in my second job.

Be joyous in what you are doing—and grateful for activity that is the real secret of success—because gratitude opens the floodgates of consciousness and leaves the way open to receive all the bounty and beautiful success that God has intended for you to have. Man was not created to struggle. He was created to manifest forth his God-Being. "To be about his Father's business."

Money

Money is the highest form of Substance that we know upon this plane. Why? Because without it everyone thinks he cannot eat, be housed, dress, or even buried. The Bible states, "The Substance of things hoped for, the evidence of things not seen."

People constantly hope for Substance but this Bible passage means that we can't see from whence it comes. But as you rise spiritually you can see that God sends us our Substance, which is never-ending.

Mary Baker Eddy, in *Science and Health*, states, "Substance is incapable of discord or decay." In other words, all real Substance comes from the Divine Mind-God. Thus the Substance of money is completely spiritual, and is incapable of making mankind a victim of poverty or lack of any kind. Fear is man's worst enemy, and so what is the answer? To not allow ourselves to fear, because when we do, we are dishonoring God. We are not believing with all our hearts and souls that God is "All in All."

Money is a wonderful thing to have if we give it its proper place in our lives. Supposing you were a great musician and were composing a sonata, would you worry about not having enough notes? Of course not. There is an unlimited supply of notes, no matter how many are using them. So you write your sonata with full confidence that notes are endless in supply. The same is true with money. The great treasure house of God contains an endless supply of good, and money is a part of that great magnificent ever-ready supply that is pouring endlessly into our hands and use. We have but to know this; feel it, love not only God but also the glorious Angels who so generously give us their help and love constantly. If you have a concept that money is hard to get, change that this instant and know that you include in your God-given Being all the money you will ever need. When a tree is planted, it certainly is not concerned that it won't have any leaves—and just think how much more God loves you as His children. The tree stands as a symbol of His love. You stand as a complete reflection of all God has to give of Himself. Claim It! Be It!

Chapter Fourteen
A Complete Change in Business

My husband has been in the finance business most of his life. But while I was "reading" him one day, I told him that he was going to be in an entirely new project, one he had never even thought of. "Well, at present," he said, "I don't know what it could possibly be. I have no prospects for a new career."

"You will have," I continued. "I see a large, low building, and many workmen. Among them is a dark-haired, young, unmarried man who will be a very necessary part of the business. Also I see several other men who will be important to you. They are married."

"That dark-haired young man has come up in my readings before, but I haven't as yet met him," answered Ben. "You have me puzzled."

A few months later the puzzle began to fit together. We have a real estate broker who has traded some of our property for us from time to time. Mr. Strand, the broker, called Ben one day and told him he had the prospects on a trade for some of our Shasta acreage. It turned out to be a private labeling business owned by a woman whose husband had passed on six years before. She was tired of running the business, with all its responsibilities. Ben and Mr. Strand met with Mrs. Unger, the owner. The meeting was not satisfactory. They could come to no agreement whatsoever. Later, Mr. Strand called Mrs. Unger, but it was still a standoff. Mr. Strand finally called Ben and told him the whole deal was hopeless—to forget it, and that he would find something else for us.

When Ben told me about this, I couldn't accept it. I sat down and did a meditation, lifting my consciousness to be in tune with God and the Angels. I was told to have Ben go by himself to see Mrs. Unger. He protested at first saying that he didn't want to go over Mr. Strand's head. I countered with the fact that the broker would receive his commission either way, since he was the finder of the deal, so it would make no difference to him.

Ben went, while I prayed. He and Mrs. Unger came to a beautiful agreement and in three weeks Ben was established in his own business, and it has been going great and building every day. The young dark-haired man turned out to be Mrs. Unger's son, who is a master mechanic. Actually, Ben says, a genius. He is playing a very important role in the business, just as was predicted.

This experience just happened a few days ago and I would be remiss if I did not tell you about it because it can help so many of you:

My husband was working on a business deal that was very difficult to close. There seemed to be obstacle after obstacle in the way. So I decided to use this decree that I learned from the "I AM" books for supply. This is the Decree: "I demand from the Treasure House of the 'I Am Presence' the constant flow of the supply of money into my (husband's) hands and use (for constructive purposes) for the fulfillment of his Divine Plan of Abundance in my (his) Life Stream." I said this out loud for about ten minutes. In an instant after I finished, the phone rang and a voice at the other end said, "Hello, Poleete. I haven't talked to you for many years. This is Mary. Eighteen years ago, when my finances were at a low ebb, you gave me some money. Now I want to repay you."

My answer was, "Mary, I don't remember about the money but I do remember that you introduced me to the *Infinite Way* by Joel Goldsmith, and I spent many happy years studying under him. He was a great teacher and metaphysician." Several other monies came to me also from unexpected sources. You can see what came from making contact with the Higher Sources that are always there for all of us!

Chapter Fifteen
Prosperity

Prosperity is in constant evidence all around you. Abundance of everything you need is in constant evidence but most people who are feeling something lacking are so busy looking at an empty pocketbook (or an empty life) that they can't see it.

Pause for a moment and think about this. When I look out of the window to the left of me I see a tree which is supplied with thousands of leaves. If I stood on my balcony and looked over the freeway, I would see thousands of cars passing daily—everywhere we look is abundance. Stores are crammed with every kind of item imaginable. Everything, absolutely everything in your lives, points to abundance.

Experts try to tell us that there is a lack of this and that—it isn't so. The sun above us is filled with all the energy we will ever need for all of eternity. This is being tapped. My husband was told by a building contractor that 60% of all of his homes now being built have solar power. Soon it will be 100%, and you can be sure other contractors are doing the same. Of course, if you accept lack in anything, you are going to have it. Lack of money, lack of companionship, lack of health, or lack of success. These seem to be the major things that people think they lack.

Let's start with money. Money does seem to talk. It says, "Without me you can't live, because you can't eat, house yourself, or clothe yourself. You can't even die because it takes me—money." Money sounds pretty conceited—but actually it is telling the truth, because in this economy, it is important.

Now what do you have to do to change your concept of money? The concept does have to be changed, whether you have a lot of it or very little. If you are wealthy, as many are who come to me for readings—then there is always a fear of losing money through dishonesty, lack of judgment or investments, or that it can be stolen. The Bible states, "The love of money is the root of all evil," but that statement has to be understood properly. It doesn't mean actual money because in spite of thinking money can talk—it can't. Actually, it talks through you. It is dead until you put it to work. What power has a $100 bill left lying in a drawer? It can't get up and walk and spend itself—you have to do that. So *you* put the power behind money. Since it is a high form of substance—*money is God in action.* How could that be the root of evil? The evil comes in loving money, hoarding it, and becoming selfish with it, fearing its loss or wasting it.

Money stands for circulation. It must be circulated properly. I had a case of a woman who was suffering from poor circulation in her arms and legs. She could hardly move. I immediately took up the thought of money. She seemed to lack it. Money came into her experience and so the circulation in her body returned. You might ask how this was done. First, I talked to this woman about accepting the right concept of money. This took some doing because her consciousness had accepted lack for so long, but at last we broke this barrier through deep prayer and meditation, and working with the right idea of supply through the Angels. Her entire life became changed because before she was blind to the truth, and it darkened her entire being. But thank God, she did see and was blessed with the light of understanding.

Now the world beliefs are trying to blind all of us and tell us there is a lack of water. There isn't. The appearance may scream that there is, but we are told in the Bible to "Judge not by appearance but to judge righteous judgment—which means to think correctly, or rightly.

Let me tell you a true incident in my own experience to prove this. I had purchased a cabin at Big Bear. This particular summer when we went there for a vacation, we were told that our well was dry. There had been such a dry winter that all the wells had run out of water, and we would have to buy any water we used in the village, where it was piped in from San Bernardino. From all outward appearance no one in our locale had any water. So I immediately went to work.

I looked up everything on water in my Bible through using the concordance. The references were plentiful. I filled my consciousness with a complete supply of water and expressed this to my family. I absolutely refused to believe in the evidence of the senses. I knew that "The earth was the Lord's and the fullness therein." The following day, after a night of prayer, a friend who liked to hike went for a walk up a steep hill. He climbed about fifty feet above our well, which was located some distance from our cabin. One other family besides ourselves had rights to this well. Now this friend I spoke about came across a damp spot of ground. He became excited and started probing with a stick; as he did so he saw a slight seepage of moisture. He ran down the hill, calling to my husband and son. They climbed eagerly up the slope with shovels, and lo and behold, they found a gushing underground stream. The following week we went back to town and purchased pipes and everything necessary to pipe the water into the cabin; before, we had to carry the water from the well. So the blessing was twofold.

One day soon after, the forest ranger came by to see our finding and he said, "I don't know what has happened, but water has sprung all over this side of the mountain. All of the cabins have water now." Of course in my work I included everyone.

Chapter Sixteen
The Growing Beans

When you surrender something, you give it up. In spiritual language, when you surrender yourself to God and the Angels, you go up by giving up your false material concepts. This type of surrender is a tremendous release from the human phase of life. The moment that you can visualize yourselves as ideas of God encased in an ever-effulgent light, then your freedom from the bondage of flesh begins. You no longer are a statistic waiting for some dire event to befall you because you were even born, such as becoming a victim of epidemics, accidents, illnesses, et cetera. Things that the false law of averages has placed upon you.

When you surrender yourselves wholeheartedly to God, then your entire life takes on a different pattern. You walk in the consciousness of your real self as inseparable from the divine.

It seems as though to most people, the easy way is to flow with the masses, but this is not so. In the long–run, it is the difficult route to take, because then your lives become fraught with various and sundry problems where there is no answer humanly. On the other hand, to follow a spiritual teaching using the knowledge of Angels, lives can become a pleasure. Each day can be a challenge to test the strength of your understanding. You can place the "Light of God that *never* fails" into every situation and in every condition. Soon you will see the darkness dissipate into the nothingness it always was.

You must surrender all personal sense in order to realize our God awareness completely. In order to feel that you are under the direction of a Divine Presence in everything you do, the relinquishment of the little ego has to come first.

When David slew Goliath with a small stone, he had surrendered himself completely to God. He knew that he couldn't conquer a big giant. He was just a small lad, but this realization and faith in God was greater than all the Goliaths in the world. He was armed with the dauntless courage that only complete reliance could give. So he was victor over the enemy.

You too can be victors, over apathy, lack of discipline, sin, sickness, and the myriad ills that are placed on mankind, but you must have absolute undeviating faith that "all things are possible to God" and the Angels. Faith that can conquer Goliaths and move mountains. There is no achievement too great, no demonstration too difficult, if you surrender your own petty human weapons to God's mighty love and power.

A few years ago I was asked to sing at the Braille Institute annual Christmas luncheon. This was always a big event for the blind. A week before the luncheon was to take place, my voice teacher, who was also my accompanist, told me that the woman who was to supply the main course for the meal had fallen ill, and there didn't seem to be anyone who had offered to fill the need. I thought for a moment while my teacher was lamenting this sad fact, then I said, "Would they like homemade beans and ham hocks, do you suppose?"

"Of course they would," answered my teacher, "if you made them, Poleete. I've eaten your cooking."

I asked how many were expected. "One hundred," she said. I gasped to myself. Twenty people were the most I had ever cooked for at one time, and that was a very special occasion.

However, I hastened home and announced the news to my husband, who only laughed and said, "Oh you'll manage somehow—I know you too well."

"I've got to," was my reply. "I can't let all those dear blind people down."

Our finances were at one of the low ebbs, so I had to think fast. A friend suggested that I go to a wholesale grocery downtown, which I promptly did. I told the manager the story and he gave me everything—beans, tomato sauce, canned tomatoes, and onions—below wholesale. He figured out how much I would need to feed one hundred people. I had no idea whatsoever. Then I went to the Grand Central Market for the ham hocks. I told the butcher the story, and he too gave me what he considered the right amount for less than wholesale.

Everything was going great. When I came home with all those supplies, I realized with dismay that I didn't have anything to cook in that would hold one-tenth of what I had purchased. I prayed, of course. That evening I told my husband my huge problem. He said, "Worry not, I have a friend in the restaurant business. I will get you a large kettle—you'll need it."

That night I soaked the beans and the next day I started on an all-day cooking job. I had to stand on a stool to reach the bottom of the big pan to stir the boiling beans and sauce. They turned out to be delicious. Of course, I tasted them, so did my husband; everything was set for the day.

My husband drove me over to the auditorium where the luncheon was to take place because he had to carry in the huge pan. The kitchen was buzzing when I got there. Ladies were making salads, cutting bread and pies—and I was stirring my beans with a long-handed ladle, kneeling on a chair to do this.

About thirty minutes later, my voice teacher came in. Her face was crestfallen. She blurted out, "Poleete, what will we ever do? There are two hundred and fifty people out there; they had to set up more tables and chairs. I told you a hundred at the most."

"Yes, I know," I said, just a little weakly, looking at my beans. Then I thought, "Well, Poleete, now is your chance to prove what you always believed, that God and the Angels could do anything. Anyway, didn't Jesus multiply the loaves and fishes?"

I turned to my bewildered teacher and said—out loud this time— "Don't you worry, this vessel holds all that we will need. You will see." The other ladies scrambled out and brought more bread, more pies and more lettuce, but I just calmly stayed, stirred, and prayed.

We started serving. I know this will sound impossible to some of you, but my blessed pot of beans never emptied, and many people asked for second servings. There wasn't anything unusual about the beans except so much love went into the making that these dear people felt it. I sang Christmas songs for them with a heart full of gratitude and joy for the goodness of God.

When I went to pick up my huge pan, the bottom was still filled. I showed my voice teacher, who marveled at the apparent miracle. On the way home she said, "Poleete, I have a young friend who has four boys. Her husband has been out of work, and I know they would love to have those delicious beans. She gave us the address and we went to the woman's house and filled a large pan with beans. I saved enough for my husband who liked them so well. Even he, who had by that time witnessed many wonderful demonstrations of the Power of God, was astounded. He always claimed that he never got accustomed to the things he saw before his very eyes that could not be denied or dismissed as accidental or coincidental. Certainly it wasn't either of those things. As I was consciously maintaining the fullness and completeness of my oneness with God (and therefore every one of those people who came to eat were also one with the Father) supply had to flow ceaselessly, and have an infinite never-ending appearance in whatever form was needed at the moment. And at this moment, it had to be just ordinary beans, well–flavored, but still beans. I also never doubted for one moment that all would be well—because I knew that it already was!

When you surrender yourselves to the "Kingdom of God that lies within," then you will know true freedom. You will no longer battle conditions, situations or people because you will know that the "battle is the Lord's," and He who created you will sustain you forever and ever.

Chapter Seventeen
Abundance

<u>A</u>bundance of Angel Power is sending
<u>B</u>lessings to
<u>U</u>nite all
<u>N</u>eighbors in that
<u>D</u>ivine Pattern that
<u>A</u>cknowledges only the re-
<u>N</u>ewal of the
<u>C</u>hrist consciousness on Earth for-
<u>E</u>ver and ever.

Abundance

We all possess it. It was given to us when we were created. Now most people, when they think of the word abundance, immediately—if not sooner—think in terms of money. It comes into the subject, but is by no means its full meaning. A farmer, for instance, when he thinks of the word, he connects it with crops; a writer thinks of words; a musician thinks of notes; a storekeeper thinks of customers. While all of these things ultimately result in supply, they are not the first thought of these people (unless, of course, they have made money their God, which is a very serious thing to do).

When I looked up the word abundance in my thesaurus, I was amazed to find at least fifty or more meanings of the word. We will go into some of them. *Greatness*, for instance, was one. I pondered this for some time, then I realized that God Himself was *abundance* because of His greatness. So then we, as we advance, can take on some of that greatness because we are a part of Him. But in order to attain even a portion of that greatness, what do we have to do? First we have to become "unselfed"— the little ego that we like so well has to go. We also have to purify our consciousness. How do we do that? By forgiving all past injustices, and also forgetting them. It doesn't do any good to forgive, and then remember past ills. We need to have only clean, uplifting thoughts, deeds, and actions, and never speak ill of anyone at any time. We need to be loving even if the love is not returned. *Purity* is the key word to greatness.

Believe it or not, one of the meanings of *abundance* was "ascend." This one I did ponder for some time. Then the bright light dawned, and I saw that as we ascend above the human rubbish of everyday living and see spiritually, that we can have an abundance of all good things—*harmony, peace, love, faith, joy, songs in our hearts, kindness, beauty* unlimited—in abundance! How wonderful!!

Then another meaning had me puzzled. *Herculean*. Just how did this fit abundance, I thought. Then I saw—Hercules stood and does stand for strength. Yes, and power.

We must have the strength of our own convictions. If by following them we make mistakes, don't stay in the mire of a mistake—have the strength to rectify it as soon as you can. Many times mistakes are stepping stones to greater wisdom. So don't wallow in self-pity. Have the courage to lift yourself up and pursue another path. Go to the Angels for guidance. They are always there and ready to aid you in every way. Awaken every morning with the Herculean strength to face a new birth—a new, wonderful, marvelous day—leave yesterday where it is. If it was joyous, be glad— if not, dismiss it because *now* is the only time, and you have it all before you to accomplish and do Herculean things—if you will.

Do you remember how Hercules was faced with unbelievable tasks? He accomplished them all because he persisted, and he also *knew* that he could do them. That is one of the great secrets—*knowing* our own abilities—our own strength to do what is given us to do. Remember His Herculean spirit is with you—use it!

Another one of the meanings of the word abundance was *importance*. This really puzzled me. So I pondered and asked the Angels for their precious help and, of course, they answered.

There are so many things; frivolous, unnecessary things, we give too much importance too. I saw how we had to regulate our daily tasks and weed out the unimportant ones. Then also, our thoughts—so much time is spent in shallow thinking, anxious thinking, useless thinking, worried thinking. Thinking about tomorrow when it isn't even here yet. So I began to sort out what was of importance, and of course, I saw that "keeping one's mind stayed on God," was of primary importance. To pray and to meditate was on the list. To keep happy thoughts and loving ones for all mankind. I could see that the abundance of all these things was of very great *importance*. And taking the word importance apart, it means to "carry within one's self"—and we should all feel our own importance as children of God, abundantly cared for by the Angels. This in itself is a thrilling thought.

Abundance also meant *unlimited*. Think of it! We are unlimited in every way, but we must accept and *know* this. People who have accomplished great things had to *know* that. The men who made it possible for our astronauts to go beyond what man could even think was reasonable had to have unlimited vision. Mankind shackles himself with his own bindings, and then blames everyone else, including God. This is pure stupidity. Don't be guilty of that. God created you perfect, with every possible opportunity to achieve. He even created the Angels to help you on your bumbling ways. And all that is asked of you is to live a pure life and realize there is something more than yourselves—a higher selfhood upon which you can call. These are Angels and beautiful glorious Ascended Masters eager and ready to aid mankind. That is their mission, and you only have to be aware of this. To *know* it with all your heart.

Another connotation of the word abundance was *remarkable*. This really stumped me. Then again I asked the Angels to open the door for me so that I could see the light and they did.

To know and to share in the abundance of all these wonderful things is in itself *remarkable*. How fortunate we are! How fortunate you are to hear this and inculcate it into your consciousness. Take a moment and think about this. Let us meditate for a moment.

Taking the word *remarkable* apart we find that "re" means to go back to. Then the word mark would mean the source. So the entire word actually means to go back to the source, and there is your *abundance*, because the *source is God*!

Noble is another meaning of the word. Again, I was puzzled and again I sought my Angel messengers for an answer. The first thing that came to me was a statement I heard given by a Christian Science lecturer when I was very young, but I never forgot it. He did not mention the source or who said it, but here it is: "*Be noble and the nobility that lies in another will rise to meet your own.*" A wonderful statement. I've used it personally, and always found that it works. So it is apparent that if one is noble, he automatically brings *abundance* of good into his own life.

The word nobility has always been associated in the minds of most people as being connected with royalty. It has a much deeper meaning than that. One of the meanings is characterized by showing high moral character. In other words, an abundance of moral fiber connected with one who lives a clean, fine, life. One who helps other people along the way, not only with things, but with kind, loving thoughts; not judging or condemning in any way—just loving—and seeing the nobility that lies in everyone. Jesus said, "The Kingdom of God lies within." So you and I have to look deeply within everyone—also ourselves.

Then I came to the word *complete*. This really confused me for awhile—then once again my Angels opened my consciousness, and I realized that when we have an *abundance* of all good, we are complete in God. And remember in the first chapter of Genesis where it states that when God completed creation He beheld it and said it was very good. He was pleased with the results. And so it was a Golden Age where only love and perfection reigned—until mankind, having been given free will, misused it. Then the mist arose, and blinded mankind to the perfection that was always there (and still is). Now it is up to us, and people like us who are studying on the right path, to help bring back a Golden Age. To some degree as we use these teachings, we can have a personal Golden Age all our own. Each day as we live this, and accept our *complete* oneness with God and all the beauty that life has to offer, we can have a Golden Age in our own experience. Yes, it takes discipline, concentration and great love, but it is worth the effort to at least get a taste of what the Golden Age could be; a peek into a glorious life that belongs to us as children of the most high God.

The words related to the word abundance are used in the Bible 102 times—abundance 60 times, abundant 12 times, abundantly 30 times, which adds up to 102 times.

Jesus said, "I came that you might have life and have it more abundantly." Life is a gift—a gift of love, and we have to treat it that way in order to have all the abundance of good and beauty it has to offer.

The following article appeared in a self-realization Magazine in September 1972, volume 42. It absolutely proves the authenticity of the Bible. I felt that my readers would appreciate this excerpt, just as I did. I share this with all my classes.

Chapter Eighteen
The Authenticity of the Bible
The Day the Earth Stood Still

National Aeronautics and Space Administration scientists in Greenbelt, Maryland, were busy recently plotting the orbits of planets—a necessary precaution when sending a satellite or rocket into interplanetary space. A satellite, once set in orbit around the sun or a planet, will remain there indefinitely unless it bumps into some other space object such as a comet, asteroid, or planet. It was that possible "bumping" which the scientists were concerned about. The space where the satellite is now moving might be uncluttered, but what about 1,000 years from now?

In order to check the accuracy of their computations, scientists were running the computer time-clock backward, potting elapsed time against the unerring motions of the planets and positions of the stars. As the computer scanned the centuries, it came to a halt. A discrepancy was indicated: either the data fed to the computer was incorrect, or the results computed to the established standards were erroneous. The program and equipment were checked, but everything was in perfect order. After further analysis, the reason emerged; the head of IBM operations telephoned NASA: "There is a day missing in elapsed time!"

Scientists on the team concluded: "*If* such an event had occurred during recorded history, it surely would have been noted somewhere." Yet nothing could be found in the annals of science. Recalling a Biblical story, a member of NASA suggested they consult the Old Testament to see if the wonder could be explained. In the Book of Joshua, the prophet said: "'Sun, stand thou still upon Gibeon; and thou, Moon, in the valley of Ajalon.' ...So the sun stood still in the midst of heaven, and hasted not to go down about a whole day" — Joshua 10:12–13.

Returning to the computer, the scientists programmed the information. The results were gratifying, but not completely so. The elapsed time in Joshua's day came to 23 hours and 20 minutes. Forty minutes were still missing! They knew time has to be accounted for, and very accurately, for any slight mistake will be multiplied by each orbit of a satellite. The total error might be multiplied a thousand or a million times during the life of the satellite. Referring again to the Biblical passage, they noted that the heavenly luminaries "hasted not to go down about a whole day."

Once again the record of the ancient prophets was consulted: "'This sign shalt though have of the Lord,...shall the shadow go forward ten degrees, or go back ten degrees?' (asked Isaiah.) And Hezekiah answered, 'It is a light thing for the shadow to go down ten degrees: nay, let the shadow return backward ten degrees.' And Isaiah the prophet cried unto the Lord: and he brought the shadow ten degrees backward, by which it had gone down in the dial of Ahaz" — II Kings 20:9–11. Ten degrees of the sun's motion represents an elapsed time of exactly 40 minutes! The day was complete.

So the story had a happy ending—for the scientists, who were relieved of the burden of inexplicable heavenly phenomena—and for the faithful, who were reassured by the infallibility of the Heavenly Computer.

Chapter Nineteen
**The Spiritual Interpretations of the 23rd Psalm
the 91st Psalm and the 121st Psalm**

1.   "THE LORD IS MY SHEPHERD, I SHALL NOT WANT."
        First of all, let us think of what a shepherd does. David, who wrote this Psalm, was a very young shepherd. A shepherd has to have a great love for his flock. He protects them, if need be with his own life. In those days of David, wild animals roamed freely and were always after the sheep for food. So a good shepherd kept alert watch.

2.   "HE MAKETH ME TO LIE DOWN IN GREEN PASTURES"
        In other words, God has made (or created) the *green pastures* for us and they are symbolic of supply. Have you ever wondered why paper money is called "greenbacks?" Because green is a symbol of growth—of all growing things. Money can grow for us if we take the limits from it. Realize when you hold a dollar bill in your hand that it symbolizes all the money in the world—*that one dollar bill*. Also green pastures stand for comfort. The soft grass makes a lovely place in which to lie. Shepherds led their flocks to green pastures for food and rest.

3.   "HE LEADETH ME BESIDE THE STILL WATERS"
        God is always giving us leading or guidance through His Angels. They are constantly pointing out the way, but we have to acknowledge them fully, ask to have this guidance revealed, and follow. Then we will

find the "peace that passeth understanding" (that is, *human* understanding) because "still waters" stand for peace and quietude. That is why meditation is so important, because we have to become "still" within as well as without. Try meditating by visualizing a still, quiet lake. See the blue of the sky reflected in the water and soft, flowing trees casting green shadows over the lake, and the sweet perfume of flowers filling the gentle breezes as they blow over your face.

4.   "HE RESTORETH MY SOUL."
        In other words, as you recognize your true Selfhood with God and His Angels, you become aware of your real Being, which is your Soul (created by God). You will have many bodies but only *One* Soul.

5.   "HE LEADETH ME IN THE PATHS OF RIGHTEOUSNESS FOR HIS NAME'S SAKE."
        The important word here is *leadeth.* A shepherd leads his flock, and the sheep follow willingly—because they instinctively know that their shepherd loves them and would only guide them rightly. Mankind, on the other hand, most of the time imposes his own will into his affairs and then wonders why he has so many problems. He blames everything and everyone else for his plight. On the other hand, we should only pray, meditate, and rely completely on the Father, and then ask for guidance. Jesus told us to *Ask* and we would receive, but our asking has to be *complete confidence* in the One Omnipotent Mind, God. Then for "His Name's Sake" will mean for us what it was intended to mean. God's *Name* is *I*—so as heirs we all bear the name of "*I.*" Other names are given to us to distinguish one from another, but in your meditation, claim with fervor that you know your name as "I." I and my Father are one.

6.   "YEA, THOUGH I WALK THROUGH THE VALLEY OF THE SHADOW OF DEATH I WILL FEAR NO EVIL, FOR THOU ARE WITH ME, THY ROD AND THY STAFF THEY COMFORT ME."
        Notice here that the important word is "through." This doesn't necessarily mean death in the sense that we think of it. It also has the connotation of walking into and "through" the death (which means end) of difficulties. Suppose, for instance, there is a thought of lack of any kind. We learned in an earlier passage that since the Lord is our Shepherd, we shall not want. Here we are told that we need fear no evil: no evil thing, no evil condition. Evil means a lack of good. We don't have to fear the situation, whatever it may be, because His rod and His staff (something upon which we can lean) is there to comfort us. What is that comfort? His Angels who have "charge over us in all our ways." If we will take the condition and use it to attain more consciousness of the "Christ" Light within us, which is always there, then the rod which we do come under only becomes a directive, and not a punishment. Many times trials appear to force us to learn

91

more about the spiritual way of life. God does not put us in these situations, we place ourselves there by some sort of Karma that has to come under the immutable law of cause and effect. It is not what we go *through* that counts, it is *how* we go through it. If we come out knowing more about God and the Angels, then the rod has been beneficial. But if on the other hand we become bitter or fearful, we build up more Karma that ultimately has to be "burned up" in this life or the next earth life.

I have walked in situations that looked insurmountable, but I always went *through* them to the *Light* beyond and learned the lessons they had to teach. It wasn't simple or easy, but I knew that comfort and love awaited me if I would see the blessing in the condition instead of the evil, or lack of good.

7.   "THOU PREPAREST A TABLE BEFORE ME IN THE PRESENCE OF MINE ENEMIES."

David knew that if we walked *through* the condition, all wonderful nutrients for the soul would be spread before us. And as the only enemy we can have is ourselves, with a table before us, set with every possible means for deliverance from the enemy, we cannot help but rise to greater heights and success!

8.   "HE ANOINTETH MY HEAD WITH OIL."

"Head" is realization of our completeness with God through *consecration* prayer and the oil of gladness. Oil stands for *consecration* and *prayer*—also for gladness or happiness.

9.   "MY CUP RUNNETH OVER."

The "cup" is your feelings, and when you receive the real meaning of this beautiful psalm, your heart brims over with the glorious realization of God's great goodness, and your oneness with Him and the Beloved Angels.

10.   "SURELY GOODNESS AND MERCY SHALL FOLLOW ME ALL THE DAYS OF MY LIFE AND I WILL DWELL IN THE HOUSE OF THE LORD FOREVER."

How could anything but goodness and mercy come into our Being if we follow the preceding verses and *live* them? "House" is consciousness. The "House" of the "Lord" is complete, and absolute reliance upon Him and His Angels for everything. Shutting the door at our "House" to all human opinions, and to human will, and dwelling the light of ever-present-love—saying constantly, "Father, not my will—but *Thine* be done."

91st Psalm

1.   "He that dwelleth in the secret place of the most high shall abide under the shadow of the Almighty."

To dwell is to live in a place. And here it is a secret place, because it is under the most high influences where nothing, nor no one, can defile it. It is kept secret, or safe, because the "Hand of the Almighty" is there as we abide, or stay in the protection of spiritual consciousness.

2.   "I will say of the Lord, He is my refuge and my fortress, my God; in Him will I trust."

Wherever we are and whatever is going on around us, we can always be assured of a refuge in God and that the Angels are fortifying our lives, if we trust with all our hearts.

3.   'Surely He shall deliver thee from the snare of the fowler, and from the noisesome pestilence."

In other words, we cannot become ensnared or made captive by any untoward condition or situation. We can feel assured of safety, even from dire diseases, if we will only realize that the "Shadow of His right hand rests upon the hour"—and is always there.

4.   "He shall cover thee with His feathers and under His wings shall thou trust; His truth shall be thy shield and buckler."

There is nothing softer than downy feathers that are under the wings of a bird, who comforts and nestles her brood to keep them warm and secure. The truth is that God is all the shield and buckler we ever need. For this is our defense against any evil.

5.   "Thou shalt not be afraid for the terror by night; nor for the arrow that flieth by day."

At night problems always seem to loom up into terrifying proportions, but if we will only turn unreservedly to God they will vanish as mist before the morning sun, and even the sharp arrow. Disturbances that try to mar our day will be blunted, and turned aside with a prayer.

6.   "Nor for the pestilence that walketh in darkness; nor for the destruction that wasteth at noon day."

We do not have to fear even those things that would try to sneak up on us when our thoughts are in a dark mood, and would try to take our days and waste them (usually in self-pity). We can turn instantly and repeat the words our Master gave us: "Get thee behind me, Satan." Because all thoughts of darkness are satanic and can be dispelled instantly by Light entering our consciousness.

7.   A thousand shall fall at thy side, and ten thousand at thy right hand; but it shall not come nigh thee."

In other words, we can never judge by appearance. Our Bible tells us that. No matter what seems to go on around you—you don't have to take it into your lives. Rise above the appearance and "look up."

8.   "Only with thine eyes shalt thou behold and see the reward of the wicked."

Actually this statement is self-explanatory. One only sees with material eyes the prosperity of a dishonest person. Just because someone, who through devious means becomes wealthy or is a cruel and selfish individual, this doesn't mean that money or success will give him peace. The only peace anyone ever really receives is through knowing God. There is no other way. Those sad people who gain through dishonesty build up Karmas that go on through many lives. It is right to have prosperity and beauty around you, but these have to be earned by devotion to God and love for one another. There is no other permanent way.

9.   "Because thou has made the Lord, which is my refuge, even the Most High, thy habitation."

In other words, you live in God. Habitation means a place you inhabit—where you abide constantly.

10.   "There shall be no evil befall thee, neither shall any plague, come nigh thy dwelling."

This statement, again, explains itself. For if we do these things and are sincere, nothing evil can really touch us.

11.   "For He shall give His Angels charge over thee to keep thee in all thy ways."

Here we definitely have proof that God created Angels for us, and they manifest His Omnipresence in our lives. They will keep us always on the path if we but acknowledge their existence.

12.   "They shall bear thee up in their hands, lest thou dash thy foot against a stone."

Hands stand for power—the power of the Angels. How wonderful to think of this great gift that Our Father has bestowed upon us just for the asking! And these beloved Angels will even remove stumbling blocks (which are the stones) from our path of Life. Think of it!

13. **"Thou shalt tread upon the lion and adder; the young lion and the dragon shalt thou trample under feet."**

The lion here stands for problems that seem vicious and ready to devour us, while the adder is the subtle thing that would seem to creep into our lives and poison our happiness. The young lion would be problems that are just trying to start, that are new ones to face. While the dragon stands for vicissitudes that have seemed to drag on for years, that appear to get larger and larger as we believe them. But here we are told that all of these so-called dire conditions can be overcome. How? By "trampling them" out of existence with spiritual "understanding" which is symbolic of "feet." Try this. Take any problem, face what it seems to be, then apply your new-found realization of your oneness with God to it, and watch it vanish into the nothingness it always was. One great spiritual leader said, "Error is the sum total of nothingness." All human problems can be erased by knowing that only what God created is real.

14. **"Because He hath set His Love upon me, therefore will I deliver Him: I will set Him on high because He hath known My name."**

The Bible is a book of promises, but we have to be worthy, and earn these promises of God. How? By loving Him with all our hearts and all our souls, above everything else: family, friends, things, and money. It isn't the fear of money that brings misery, but the love of it. Many people unwittingly put money before everything. Then they wonder why they are so unhappy. Money is necessary, but it has to be put into its proper place. God must be first, then supply will follow in abundance, and we will be delivered from lack, from disease of any nature because we become aware of His name as "I." We have learned from the explanation of the 23rd Psalm that our real names are also "I"—because we are children of God.

15. **"He shall call upon me and I will answer Him. I will be with Him in trouble and I will deliver Him and honor Him."**

All God asks is that we call on Him, but this has to be done with fervor and complete dependence. The little ego "i" has to be completely dispelled. Then He will not only deliver us, but also honor us with His love through our beloved Angel Beings.

16. **"With long life will I satisfy Him and show Him my salvation."**

If we abide, dwell, and believe, then we are given an understanding that life is continuous and forever. Through salvation which means to be saved, we become safe from all manner of problems, and when they do appear we have a solution that never fails, because the "Light of God never fails." For "underneath are the Everlasting Arms"—of Love.

121st Psalm

1.   "I will lift up mine eyes unto the hills from whence cometh my help."

This is lifting up your consciousness to a high state, instead of staying down in the mundane mess of a so-called problem. The instant that we look above and beyond the appearance of anything unlike God, that instant our healing takes place. We may not see the results at once, but they are there where the problem seemed to be, and you will soon be aware of the power of your right thinking.

2.   "My help cometh from the Lord which made heaven and earth."

Actually there is no line of demarcation between heaven and earth. They are the same, because we make our own heaven by dwelling in the "house of the Lord," which is again our own Consciousness. "The earth is the Lord's and the fullness therein," we are told. We are the Masters over conditions. If everyone would become conscious of this for one instant, there would be no smog, for instance. Smog is the result of wrong thinking. Oh yes, many material causes are attributed to its being there, but this is not so. God didn't create it, so actually it doesn't exist. Only what God creates is true.

I proved this some time ago when I was working on a newspaper in the southern part of Los Angeles where the smog seemed to be so thick. Every morning as soon as I arrived in a certain area, my eyes started watering and I was generally very uncomfortable. One day I woke up to the fact that I was accepting this condition into my own consciousness. I knew better, but like many of us, I just endured it. But on this particular day I decided that whatever appeared outwardly had to be in my thinking—so I proceeded to think correctly. I knew that smog could never be in the Kingdom of God, and that was where I actually dwelt. I said it every day, so I had to live it. From that moment to this, I have never been bothered by smog. When other people mention it to me, I realized that I wasn't aware of it even existing, so consequently there were no unhappy results. God created good, pure air. Accept that, and you will have it. After I had had this experience, God and the Angels placed me on this beautiful hill where the air is as clear as I knew it to be.

3.   "He will not suffer thy foot to be moved; He that keepeth thee will not slumber."

4.   "Behold He that keepeth Israel shall neither slumber nor sleep."

The word "suffer" in the archaic means "to allow." God will not *allow* our spiritual understanding to be changed, because all He knows about us is spiritual. We are the ones who take ourselves off the path. We allow ourselves to stray. God is always aware—of course He doesn't "slumber." He is aware of our oneness with Him. We are His beloved children.

5.   **"The Lord is thy keeper; the Lord is thy shade upon thy right hand."**

What greater assurance can we have than these beautiful words: that the Lord is our keeper. Enfold yourselves in that marvelous realization. You are never alone when you know this. His beloved, precious Angels surround you constantly. The shade on your right hand is protection and power. The "hand" stands for power.

I remember once I was working for a man spiritually who was facing a serious charge. The day for his arraignment came. I was given the exact time that he would appear in the courtroom. I knew the man to be completely innocent of the charges against him, so as I sat praying, I worked with the thought from the Bible, "The shade of His right hand rests upon the hour." I stayed with that one statement and, needless to say, the whole case was dismissed. Everyone connected with it was amazed, including this man's wife, who had called me for help. The man was not a strong believer at all, but his wife was, and so he benefited. We can use that statement for anything that appears to be erroneous. Just knowing that our Father, God, never forsakes us, gives us confidence to face anything.

6.   **"The sun shall not smite thee by day nor the moon by night."**

The sun is our friend. It gives life to all living things. I once heard about a man who was a surveyor. He was sent into the desert to do some surveying and, of course, he had to walk. It was a hot day when he started out, but he was accustomed to the desert, and his canteen was filled with water (so he thought). After walking twenty miles or so from the closest town, he felt thirsty, and when he reached for his canteen, he found it had leaked and he hadn't a drop of water left. This man knew how "to think" in the Truth. He was a student of metaphysics, so he didn't panic, but started walking back the twenty miles and, with each step, would say, "I'm all right now—I'm all right now." He finally arrived back at his destination with no signs or appearance of fatigue or thirst. People who heard about this couldn't believe it—but it was true. Why? Because this man knew that the sun could not smite him—he had faith and understanding.

As for the "moon by night," it is the poor harmless moon which we have seen so clearly now, and even placed men upon it. But in those ancient days, when this text was written, the people believed that if you slept under the moon's direct rays, you could become insane. That is where the term "lunacy" came from, "luna" meaning "moon" in Latin. Now, of course, we know that the rays of the moon are borrowed light from the sun. Naturally they can have no effect whatever. Those old beliefs were based entirely upon superstition—just as our modern astrology is today.

7.   "The Lord shall preserve thee from all evil; He shall preserve thy Soul."

The Lord God is always with us. He created us from His own Being. He is our Father and our Mother. To preserve means to keep whatever it is in its original state, so God keeps us always as His Beloved Children, safe, secure in His precious arms. Since Soul is a synonym of God, He would naturally preserve it forever; because God is forever and ever. There is no such thing as a beginning or an ending. The Kingdom of God is always within us. We have but to know this and dwell within it with the glorious Angels.

8.   "The Lord shall preserve thy going out and thy coming in from this time forth and even for evermore."

This text is self-explanatory if we but examine what it means. To begin with, anything that is preserved is kept safe from spoilage or harm. If everyone would use this statement before entering a car, before a business conference, or before a trip of any kind, and really allow oneself to become so imbued with the knowledge that God and the Angels are there forever guiding, guarding, watching, and loving, affairs of every name and nature would run much more smoothly and harmoniously. It is all there for our constant use—don't leave it in a book—declare constantly your heritage with God, and you shall have it.

Chapter Twenty
The Story of William
Red Sea

The following episode in my life was just another powerful proof of the potency of God and His Angels, if we will not believe and use the truths we learn correctly.

This young man, whom we will call William, came to me with a problem that looked insurmountable. He had been accused of grand larceny and was out of jail, having paid a huge bail bond.

He was completely innocent, but the evidence stacked against him was unbelievable. He was a victim of a very sharp operator who used William's keen business knowledge, gave him a flattering title as president of the company, and proceeded to work shady business deals behind William's back. Another "slick" operator, whom we will call Joe, came well recommended to William. His family background was one of high report. He was a very well educated college man, and William, believing what he heard and saw on the surface, did not delve into any of Joe's past business tactics, which proved to be a fatal mistake on William's part.

But William had no reason to suspect Joe. He met his family and friends, and so far there was nothing to judge him by except good reports. In all of their personal dealings together, Joe seemed filled with integrity and had a good business sense. But it was in the wrong direction, which William learned about later, much to his complete dismay and sorrow. He was the victim, of course, along with others, who also knew nothing of Joe's underhanded dealings, but they too were caught up in the same tide.

When William came into my experience, the cloud had hung over his head for several years. He had no funds left. Thousands of dollars had gone into the pockets of attorneys. His case was to come up again in a few months and he had no recourse but to use the public attorney to plead his cause.

Everything seemed to be against him. The district attorney was really out to "get" Joe , and since William and the others were in the way, they too would be victims. And because William had been the president of the company, his sentence would naturally be a harsh one and a long one. William was facing what appeared to be a "Red Sea" that would take a miracle to part. And a miracle did.

William and I started working together almost daily. He was completely new in the study of metaphysics, but was eager to learn. "Man's extremity is God's opportunity." This certainly proved so. William was a conscientious student. We proceeded slowly, however, because one has to learn to crawl before he can walk, and walk before he can run. This is true in spiritual study as well as any other department of life. And when one has lived a completely materialistic life for many years, the process of teaching has to be gradual.

I, of course, worked on his case constantly. I felt the importance of seeing William free and also lift up the entire situation. As for Joe, I knew that in spite of his father's wealth, that he, being guilty, would have to "pay the piper" in full.

My first lesson with William was to help him get over his terrible resentments to those in the law who had been so unjust. So we took the name of all of them and worked daily on spiritualizing each one in our consciousness. The district attorney seemed to be the worst offender, so we gave him extra time and effort. Like magic, he changed toward William, not to the point of being benevolent, but at least his attitude softened. These people connected with the case will never know what happened to them, but the difference, William explained to me, was very marked. Even the bail bondsman to whom William owed a considerable sum of money, and who was noted for his hardness, told William not to worry about it, that they would work out something later. (We also spiritualized his name.) Along with the spiritualizing of the names, I wrote daily letters to the Angels for William and everyone connected with the situation. (Incidentally, the bail bondsman was later paid in full, of course.)

Then after about ten months of sincere effort and devotion to his study, William was faced with the final trial where the verdict would be given. This time William was armed with the truth and ready. All the human indications were that he was facing a ten-year jail term. We talked the night before the trial and I assured him "all was well."

The verdict for Joe was a ten-year stay, but for William it amounted to a few weeks—just a "slap on the wrist," as it was.

A few months after he served the five weeks, his case was reviewed and he was given a complete "clean bill of health" and the whole affair was expunged from his record.

The "Red Sea" had parted, indeed, because the Angels were there to do it. William's life ever since has been a steady climb in the business world and more important, he is as devoted a student as I have ever had and is now capable of helping others. "Love certainly entertained an Angel unawares."

Always, always remember that what can be done for another can be done for you—just "seek and ye shall find!" The power to use this Angel Power is within *you*.

Chapter Twenty-one
The Metamorphosis of Mark

This facet of my life is probably the most difficult one I have ever written because of the traumatic period that I experienced at this time, yet I cannot with good conscience leave it unsaid, for I feel sincerely that it can and will help others to overcome a similar problem.

Mark, my husband at the time, as I explained in an earlier chapter, was a very humanly brilliant man. He probably had more information at his fingertips than anyone I have ever met or known.

I used to call him a "walking encyclopedia." His human mind was brilliant, so he was able to digest humanly every spiritual study that I went into. He studied the Bible assiduously and could probably have preached a sermon on any text in it—and very convincingly, too. At first I was impressed at his quick knowledge of metaphysics and very pleased, but then I realized, to my dismay, that it was all in his head, not in his heart. He didn't live one sentence that he studied so earnestly. He talked it well, but that was the end of it. He lived every moment of his life exactly as he wanted to, taking no one into consideration at all. I was just there.

When money started rolling in from an invention of his, he spent it like water. After a hundred thousand dollars had gone down the drain, I insisted that my name be put on the royalties, and finally through prayer and effort, the attorney (who was Mark's friend) finally put my name on the invention so that any monies spent would have to bear my signature, as well as Mark's. In this way a certain balance was maintained on the idle spending.

But Mark continued going to his cocktail parties and staying out late at night. His disposition hadn't improved any, either. Naturally I thought of divorce many times, but every time I mentioned it to him he would practically explode, and would maintain that he loved me. I'll admit that this was rather difficult to believe, but I stayed. Until one day I realized that I had to be freed of the situation completely, so I calmly found an apartment for myself and moved out of the place where we were living together. Mark was very surprised and suggested that he move with me, but I said no, flatly and conclusively, and I told him I wanted to live alone for a while—to think.

He visited me every day, and was very attentive, but I refused his plea to move in with me. Finally, one day he came over very ill. I had two bedrooms so I put him to bed and cared for him, naturally giving him treatments, as I had done before when he was sick. Mark was very receptive to spiritual treatments, and in a short time he recovered. Then he begged to come "home" and live with me, as he called it.

Suddenly I saw Mark as a child. Not outwardly, but inwardly. It struck me with a great impact that he had never matured inside. He was a large, well-built man in appearance, but very, very immature emotionally. He needed a mother image, and I was it.

Of course I went to God and the Angels constantly about everything in my life—so this time, before I gave him an answer, I opened my Bible at random and my eyes fell on a passage that said, "Stand and see the glory of the Lord." Then I knew what I must do. It came like a great illumination in my consciousness. I had been thinking of Mark as a human man, with human frailties and a perplexing personality, when all the time he needed to be treated like one would a child who needed a great deal of love and understanding. I had to get myself out of the way with my hurt pride and hurt feelings and start on a whole new path with him. I had to have the metamorphosis first, which I did in "the twinkling of an eye." It was a magnificent revelation, and one for which I have been ceaselessly grateful ever since. God and the Angels gave me each step I was to follow. It was all set before me in vivid colors.

I didn't tell Mark what was revealed to me, but I did tell him that he could move in with me. He came that night with all his belongings, including his beloved cat, Callie.

Then began one of the most beautiful and rewarding experiences of my entire life. The change in Mark was so profound that there are no words to describe it in full. He admitted that he knew nothing about spiritual things, really—only the letter. Then he began a study on his own in Self-Realization, a fellowship founded by Paramahansa Yogananda. He attended the church regularly, sent for the lessons, and humbly asked questions. He only had one fit of temper, and instead of answering or speaking at all, I sat quietly on the couch and kept declaring that only the presence of God was in the room and it was filled with love.

That ended even his critical remarks. His entire demeanor changed. I took over all financial matters completely. The checking accounts were put in my name only. Mark was pleased to do this, he said it relieved him of any sense of responsibility because he wanted to start writing again. In less than a year, Mark's healing was complete. He was an entirely new man, just as though he had been born again. He became the man that I saw when I first met him. The true Mark, stripped of all that was not real. Each day there appeared some new and beautiful facet of his character. He became kind, thoughtful, gentle and diligent. We spent a great deal of time together in study. For the first time, he became a real companion in every way.

Incidentally, I too was healed of ever beholding anything but the perfect man of God's creating. It gives one a great feeling of joy and true bliss to be able to experience this; it is a profound love for everyone and everything. Mark began to make different friends who believed as we did. Then he met Ben (my present husband).

Ben, when Mark first met him, was just catching glimpses of a metaphysical way of thinking. Ben is Italian, and had been reared in the Catholic faith, although he did not embrace it after he was grown. He married his first wife in her Protestant Church, and thereafter followed no religion.

When Ben met Mark, he and his wife had been apart for some time. Circumstances caused him to feel very bitter toward all women (his mother excepted, of course), so he told Mark that he had no desire to meet me. He and Mark met every Sunday for breakfast and went to the Self-Realization Church together. Ben would question Mark about religion, but Mark, by that time, realized that he didn't have all the answers as he once thought. This friendship continued for almost a year.

One day Ben was particularly intent on some answers to his questions, and Mark said, "Again, I tell you, Ben, my wife can give you the answers, I can't." Ben then decided to "break the ice" and come to see me. For the first thirty minutes of our meeting he was very reticent and withdrawn. He sort of had a tongue in cheek attitude, but in a short while he was sitting on the edge of his chair listening intently. His whole demeanor changed completely.

Many wonderful fulfilling months followed. The three of us studied together every Sunday after church. We ate together, laughed together and learned together. Mark was in "seventh heaven." Ben became his closest and best friend. After the first time I met Ben, he stopped smoking. I just said, when he lighted up a cigarette, "You don't need that, you know."

We both laughed and he replied, "I guess I really don't." He put out the cigarette and never smoked again. He told me afterward that he had smoked for years, cigars, pipe and cigarettes—and thought he never wanted to give them up. Ben, however, is a very disciplined person. He is strong and determined. I, of course, told him as he put the cigarette out, that I would work for him. He said from that moment on he never wanted to smoke again.

Benone (we call him Ben) is a handsome, slender man with dark eyes and dark hair. He is the same height as Mark was, but opposite in coloring and build. They complemented one another so well.

Mark continued to develop by leaps and bounds. He loved my Angel classes, as I mentioned in my first book, and said he learned from each of them. Ben started attending the Angel sessions, too, and he also stated that with each one he developed more understanding.

Mark constantly expressed gratitude for his change of consciousness. No one had to tell him; he knew by the inner feeling he had and by the joy that had come into his life. He talked about it continually with such happiness beaming from his handsome face, that everyone who met the "new man" remarked about it. It was especially apparent to my family and friends who had known him before the transformation.

Mark was penitent over his past mistakes, but he was not morbid over them. He worked at making his life as exemplary a one as possible. The wonderful part of it all is that he succeeded.

Marvelous, happy, fulfilling months passed, until one day Mark became very ill. He asked me to call Ben, which I did, and Ben came over in about ten minutes. By that time Mark was unconscious and passed away in Ben's arms. Mark's last words to me were, "I love you." He knew that he was passing. I thanked God over and over that Mark had had the complete enlightenment before he made the change. This realization helped me over the difficult and sad months that followed.

I had to draw on every bit of spiritual knowledge that I had ever learned. My dear friend, Anne, came every night and slept beside me. Ben, whose grief was great because he, too, loved Mark, became a Rock of Gibraltar for me. He attended to all my business affairs, and straightened out many tangled threads that took his kind of intelligence and patience and knowledge of legal affairs.

God and the Angels certainly sent Ben into my experience, because we needed each other so much. In a little less than a year after Mark's passing, Ben and I were married.

Chapter Twenty-two
The Angels Find Beth and John a Home

"The miracle that you promised, Poleete, has come to pass," was the comment I heard on the phone from Beth, whose voice was ringing with joy. "The Angels have done it again. You kept telling me that I would have my own home, but really, after four years of living in a three-room, very small, cramped apartment with four children, at times, unless you kept my spirits going, I'd have given up entirely. What with my three romping busy boys and one not too quiet girl, the prospect of at last having a huge fenced-in yard has left me almost dizzy with delight."

I was thrilled with her news, but I knew that in spite of the obstacles that loomed so large against their owning a home, that before the summer was out, some way it would come about.

Beth is one of those young women who has been blessed with a beautiful disposition to match her very beautiful face, and a patience beyond all words.

Beth has attended my Angel Classes for several years, and I have been the practitioner for her children, even before they were born. She was able to bring all of them to my last Angel Class, and they were very quiet and listened intently.

The two oldest boys, six and seven, use the Angel prayers for everything. If they lose anything, they go at once to the Angels, and the lost object is always found. They truly believe. If they don't feel well, they call me at once and say, "Nana Pete (that is what they have named me) I need you to pray for me." They all attend Sunday School, and the two boys know the Lord's Prayer by heart. It won't be long before the girl knows it too. She is only four now.

Going back to the miracle of the house, the reason it looked like "Mission Impossible" was because John had not had a steady job for three years, and they had absolutely no credit rating whatsoever. So to own a house seemed as improbable as anything could ever be. But I know and have always known that "nothing is impossible to God." If we stand firmly enough and never waver, no matter how long it seems to take, the results will always be on the positive side, because the power of good far outweighs any so-called power of evil or negativity. This, I knew, was a Karmic condition, and it had to be erased. Beth and her husband also learned while waiting. John did odd jobs and in the four years they had miraculously saved enough for a substantial down payment on a house.

On a Tuesday I called Beth and told her that I dreamed that she was moving into her own home. Beth's answer was, "Well, if you dreamed it, Poleete, it's bound to happen. I don't know how, but I do have faith that it will."

That very next Friday, they went out looking again. They told the real estate agent their huge problem, and fortunately she understood it only too well. She showed them several houses, and finally they saw one they liked that suited all their needs. "Yes," said the agent, "this is a nice house, and meets the price you can pay. And it also has a G.I. takeover plan, but four other people are in line for it."

Beth called me and told me the story in detail. "It shall be your house," I said confidently.

"Oh, I want to believe you, but it doesn't seem possible," cried Beth.

"All right, you wait and see," I answered.

A week later the agent called Beth and said, "If you want that house, hurry over. The other four people can't come up with a sufficient down payment and you people can."

Needless to say, Beth and John went at once, signed the necessary papers, paid the money, and the home was theirs. Every detail of the house was as Beth had dreamed. It is in a nice neighborhood with fine schools nearby. It has a lovely garden, already planted with flowers and trees. The house itself is large and roomy, completely carpeted with brand new carpet, and a large swimming pool. The people who owned it put a great deal of love there so the vibrations are very good. See what Angel Power can do if we but use it!

I am certain now that John will find permanent employment because the Karma has certainly been reduced considerably.

Chapter Twenty-three
The Angels Locate Lost Money

Doris is the housekeeper for a dear friend of mine. I've met Doris on occasions when I have been in my friend's home. Doris is a very lovely person and deeply religious. I have had calls from her from time to time for treatments for her brother who was healed of a serious heart condition. This time Doris called to tell me that she had lost or misplaced a considerable sum of money. I had taught Doris to write to the Angels. So this time I suggested that she turn completely to prayer. I assured her that the money would be found.

Several months passed and the lost money had not turned up. However, I kept telling Doris to not despair, that the Angels were on the job and the money would be in her hands before long. One day she called me and in a very happy voice said, "I found the money in a very unlikely place, but there it was—all of it. Those Angels certainly do work, all right—and I am very grateful." So was I. For each thing that I see, each answered prayer is always a new miracle to me, and a joyous one, even though I know that it is going to happen.

Chapter Twenty-four
My Meditation Group Lecture

Every Saturday at one in the afternoon, we met to meditate and discuss different subjects that make life a little easier to live. The group consisted of about twenty people from all walks of life. Each person had the privilege of speaking or asking for help for someone who was in need. We have had some marvelous healings from these meditation groups.

I chose a subject, either a Bible explanation by request, or a topical subject of the day. One of my topics was on the thought of fear. I will relate it here because it may help someone who is gripped by fear:

People all over the world seem to be in the clutches of fear at some time or another. There is a whole philosophy of fear being fed through the press, and over the radio and through television. It can unnerve an otherwise thinking person to the point of almost paralysis. People become afraid to do anything because they can't see what the future will hold. They come to me every day filled with frustrations and lack of direction. If they accept the spiritual, we can always work things out, but of course everyone is not ready to turn their life and affairs over to God and His Angels. So we try to help them with a reasoning course of action.

Fears know no boundaries; first we are told prosperity will come, and following that comes what fear–mongers say will be an inevitable inflationary period. Then the ax falls because "they say" a depression will have to follow. And if enough people believe it—it will happen.

Fear always has to have a form—a word. There must always be

something to fear or the word wouldn't exist. I saw headlines screaming on the front page of a newspaper that food prices were rising to an all–time high. But on the very back page of this same newspaper I read, in one small paragraph written by a brave journalist, that food prices had risen, but salaries had gone up three times as much.

Stop and think of this. America is a great country. Our ancestors pioneered through untold deprivations and dangers to build it, and we have the finest luxuries of any country in the world. Everything possible of a fearful nature has been faced already by these intrepid ancestors of ours and actually we have nothing left to really fear.

Look to your Bible; in Isiah 41:10,13 it states: "Fear thou not for I am with thee; be not dismayed for I am thy God. I will strengthen thee, yea I will help thee, yea I will uphold thee with the right hand of my righteousness."

Then in Joshua 1:9 it says, "Be strong and of a good courage, be not afraid, neither be thou dismayed, for the Lord thy God is with thee withersoever thou goest."

Begin right now to enter into a personal relationship with God. Make it a matter of daily acknowledgment, "I and my Father are one, so I will turn to the Father every hour of every day realizing that the Father and His Angels are always with me."

When you state this with all your heart, you will find your good flowing forth abundantly, and it will return to you in great waves of happiness, prosperity and the "peace that passeth understanding."

You cannot possibly fear and love God at the same time. The Bible states: "Perfect love casteth out fear." That is of course love for God and all He stands for.

Let us think of the word responsibility. We are God's responsibility as He created us after his own likeness. Our work is to respond to the ability of the Divine Father. How do we respond to God? By not building more Karma in the wrong direction, by making ourselves pure in every way. Pure from malice, envy, bad thinking about anyone, by obeying the laws of God and man and not taking into our consciousness any negativity whatsoever. If it tries to invade or take over the thinking, dismiss it at once with a prayer or a statement of truth.

Knowing God and the Angels personally is worth all the effort you can put forth. Hundreds of my students can personally attest to this.

Stay in that "secret place of the Most High." "Interiorize your thinking by meditation." Our tomorrows are created by what we do today, and what we *think* today.

Meditation has to be an experience of your very own. We cannot take the experiences of others and make them ours. It has to be individual. Know during your meditation that since God created you, He is going to maintain you. God is the substance of your being and constitutes the substance of all things: your home, your business, and your talents are all under the supervision of God, and this realization can bring the Power of Angels into your lives. You attract to you whatever your consciousness is. And if you become aware of the omnipotence, omnipresence, and omniscience of God during your meditation, and then take it into your everyday life, you can "ask what you will and it shall be done unto you." We must keep our "conversation (as well as our thoughts) in heaven." If you are not outwardly demonstrating the results of your meditations, there is something amiss in the procedure.

Search yourself thoroughly and be certain that no sense of self has entered your consciousness. You must strip off the layers of materiality, and live in the knowledge that God is all in all. If you have made the mistake of turning to the human element and created discord in your life, now is the time to turn and say, "Well, if I give this discord life, then it will be real, so I withdraw all reality from it this instant! I command my life to move in more perfect channels through God's Infinite Power. I will constantly express gratitude for the ability given to me by Divine Love to lift myself from a Karmic pattern."

The instant you become consciously aware of the presence of God as being always with you, then everything that the presence stands for comes into your experience. But we have to put this into action ourselves. No one can do it for you. True, you can be helped by another, but eventually it all depends upon the individual. Then the very miracle of life itself becomes vividly apparent.

To meditate properly, sit on a wool blanket; keep your back erect and away from the back of the chair. Your feet should also be on the woolen blanket. Your eyes must be focused on the center of your forehead (the space between the eyes). Your hands must rest on your thighs, with the palms facing upward. You should be completely relaxed and at ease. Breathe slowly from the diaphragm in and out five times, or longer if you wish. This will prepare you for a deep meditation. Be sure that you are in a quiet place. Lift your thinking God-ward and to the Angels. Keep practicing. Good and beautiful results will definitely follow.

Chapter Twenty-five
Marriage

Marriage is a beautiful word when its true meaning is understood and lived. It actually is the blending of two personalities into a oneness. It cannot be entered into lightly. When two people plan a marriage, it should be with the consciousness of it lasting as long as both shall live.

During an interview recently with a young couple who were planning a wedding in which I was going to participate as the minister, the young groom-to-be said something to me which I shall never forget, because no one had ever told me this before. With great earnestness he said, "I'd like our marriage to last as my grandmother's and grandfather's has, who have just celebrated their fiftieth anniversary."

This, of course, was a marvelous beginning for the couple. They were starting with the right concept. In marriage there is a period of adjustment. It's like two chemicals mixing; it takes time. Each has to learn to understand the other's needs and bend with the situation. Through life, in dealing with others it is important to try to see what other people feel and think, so in marriage it is doubly important in order to communicate properly, to realize how your mate feels about things. We can't always judge by our own thoughts; another's has to be considered and taken seriously. If more people would do this and talk over their particular problems, the divorce rate would be cut in half.

There are very, very few hopeless situations. It is also wise to consult a good understanding marriage counselor if you cannot solve your difficulties. A third person, especially one who is on a spiritual path, can sometimes see instantly what is the solution for a good marriage.

Living together without a marriage license is never the answer. That only leads to a Karmic situation that ultimately has to be corrected. In the chapter on Karma, you learn that any deviation from the Law of God is punished, and that is an irrevocable law.

A beautiful marriage, where each one is giving to the other equally, is perhaps the most heavenly state anyone can experience on this earth. Angels are always in attendance at every wedding ceremony, because the occasion is so beautiful when two people combine their lives and their love.

Chapter Twenty-six
Release

Release! According to the dictionary the word release means to set free, liberate. To deliver from worry, pain, obligation—to free from something that holds, that binds, to permit the circulation, sale, performance. To release also means to relax.

So to be released from the tensions of everyday living we have to learn to relax. How is this done? Through meditation. There is no better way.

When you sit down to meditate, you should release all of your so-called worries and distresses. If you do this often enough, you will find the tensions growing less each day—and your entire life will have a different meaning. But while you are releasing yourself, be sure you are releasing everyone else because if we hold anyone in bondage, then we ourselves are bound.

Many, many things have to be released in life. We cannot bind another with thoughts of sickness, drunkenness, dope addiction, or any of the errors that would seem to beset mankind. Our children have to be released at whatever age they are.

I remember a very important incident in my own life. My son was just a small boy, and he seemed to develop a very severe cough. My young husband had purchased tickets for the opera on this particular evening, and had also purchased a beautiful white satin gown for me, a pink velvet cape, and shoes to match. I was of course very eager to attend the opera with him and to wear my new outfit, but I couldn't bear the thought of leaving my baby in spite of the fact that we had a live-in housekeeper who was very capable. But my heart kept turning to my son, and every time he coughed, I felt that I should not leave him, but I also could not disappoint my husband. He was a good father, but he would not understand why I felt so bound when we had such a reliable girl to look after our son.

So I turned unreservedly to God and the Angels. Ronnie was in bed by then, but the coughing continued. I went into John's study, which was next to my son's room, and I declared out loud that he was God's son and that I released him completely to God.

My prayers were deep and sincere. In a few moments Ronnie stopped coughing and was fast asleep. This was the beginning of my release as a clinging mother—and also the release for Ronnie. I still loved him and cared for him the same as before, but not with that overwhelming molding kind of love that smothers and takes away the joy of having a child to raise.

A great lesson was learned because when I had to face different facets of my life as a mother, this incident prepared me. And whenever I began to "mother-smother," I told God that Ronnie was His son, and I meant it. As a result, Ronnie and I have always had a happy rapport because he never, even to this day, feels bound to me in any way. We enjoy one another's company when we do see each other, and there is nothing that he can't discuss with me because he knows I will not judge him. Advise, yes, when it is necessary, and he knows that he can take or leave the advice without my being upset one way or another. He is an individual child of God and he has a perfect right to work out his own Karma. Most of the time he will take my suggestions because he knows that these things come to me intuitively, but sometimes he chooses to go his own path, which is his right.

Everyone is entitled to this right, as long as he or she is not harming anyone. Then, of course, it becomes another subject entirely.

So often in marriage wives will bend a husband, making demands on his time that through business obligations he cannot fulfill. I know a case like that where the wife set the exact time for her husband to be home for dinner. If he was not there at the exact time, she had the family eat without him. In his line of business, many times clients kept him occupied. He explained this but the wife refused to speak to him the entire evening because he was late to dinner. This tactic of the wife's spilled over into other sequences of their lives.

For instance, the wife set a rule that Sunday belonged to the family. This was certainly understandable. The family unit is an important integral part of marriage, and while children are growing, they need both parents. That's for sure, but at times this young husband had business that took him out of town and this always caused a problem in the marriage.

The inevitable finally happened. This young man longed to be free

116

from any bondage, to be released, as it were. So he left the confines of the home and found an apartment for himself so that he could come and go without any shackles whatsoever. He supports his family and has left them in a lovely, comfortable home. But sadly, he is gone and has no intention of ever returning. I cannot fully justify his actions, because it always seems to me that a marriage is sacred, and that it can be worked out if both parties try hard enough. There are exceptions, of course. Unfortunately, since this husband was so bound, he is relishing his freedom now. If wives will only learn to release their husbands in the right way and try to understand more.

The same works for husbands. They too have to learn to release their wives and allow them the same freedom they desire. Not the freedom to be unfaithful, that breaks the marriage vow completely; but the freedom to come and go without a feeling of restraint. Marriage should be based on happy companionship and a feeling of sharing, but with no tangled webs of jealousy involved.

In the wedding ceremony, we ministers use the words "Holy matrimony," and that is what marriage should be. Holy means whole or complete, and for a completely harmonious union, each one must feel released, bound only by the beautiful ties of an enduring love.

I let my meditation group choose what subject they wish me to use for my sermon on Saturdays. They chose this one on "release," and it was a good one, because we all need to be released from our own selves and reach for the highest concepts that our consciousness can attain.

Release everything to God in your experiences. The Bible states: "Cast your burdens upon the Lord." When you do this, actually you then have no burdens. But this has to be done with one's whole heart and not just with your lips or your thoughts.

I remember an experience that I went through some time ago in my life. In that particular sequence of my marriage with Mark, our finances were at a very low ebb, and our credit rating was zero. I needed a new car very much as I lived on a hill, and transportation was limited. Mark was away a great deal and I had no way to get places except through friends, and most of them worked during the day.

However, one of my friends offered to sign the credit papers for me because her credit was good. I could use my old car for a down payment and, of course, I would be making the monthly payments. This sounded very kind, so the friend and her husband went with me to purchase a new small car. They both signed, and I drove home happily in my nice shiny car. Twenty-two months went by and I made all of the payments on the car. Sometimes finances were such that I was late, but very seldom. My contract was drawn up for three years. I took excellent care of the car, had it lubricated when necessary, and after twenty-two months it was almost like a brand new automobile.

During this time, my friend who had signed, had a daughter who had reached the age of twenty-two and wanted to leave home and find a place for herself. The daughter talked it over with me, and I thought it was a good idea for her to leave the "nest," as it were, and find herself. Her mother and father became infuriated at the idea and they blamed me entirely for encouraging their twenty-two-year-old daughter, who still slept in their room on a cot, to go out into the world. The daughter, whom I will call Lucy, was a beautiful, talented girl, and she wanted to find a job and have her own young friends, which she was not allowed to do. Lucy left and moved into her own place which she had found with another young woman.

About a week later, one morning I went out to get into my car and it was gone. My first thought was of course that it had been stolen. I called the police and a young officer came right over and filled out the report. When I told Lucy about it she said, "My parents took your car, Poleete. That's the sort of thing they would do."

"No," I protested, "I can't believe that anyone could possibly sink that low. They were so kind to sign for me and everything!"

"You don't know them," countered Lucy.

I found that she was right. Three days later, the young police officer came back. His face was grim. He said, "Well I've seen some rotten things, but this one beats them all." Then he went on to explain that he spotted my car and pulled the driver over to the curb. The driver, who was Lucy's father, showed the officer that the car was in their names, which it was. But I had already shown the officer my twenty-two returned checks which proved that the car was really mine.

"Say, lady," said the officer, "if you want to make a case out of this, I'll back you up all the way."

"No," I answered, "I'm going to have to handle this in my way. Thank you just the same."

"I'll be around if you need me," he said as he left.

I sat down on my couch, stunned. It was really beyond my comprehension that anyone would ever do such a thing—but here it was facing me. I knew from past experiences that things happen to teach us lessons. If we don't learn, those lessons are repeated through many lives. What must I learn from this? I asked myself. Then the answer came, "to love more." I saw what I must do, and that was to bless these poor people who would allow themselves to do such a thing over such a small incident. By doing this, they have lost their daughter forever. She has never really forgiven them. But I did. Every day I blessed these people. I sent love to them because they needed it so badly. Of course I missed having a car, but I knew that God and the Angels would provide for me and they did, through my son.

One day he called me from Big Bear where he lived and said, "Mom, I just took over a used–car lot up here and I have a dandy little car for you—and it's blue. Come and get it."

My friend Anne drove me up. Ron handed me the pink slip, saying the car was a gift. I've never loved a car so much. It even had air-conditioning in it and was in perfect condition in every way. Now what happened? I released the whole situation into God's hands and He did provide for me. Also I blessed those who seemed to be enemies and with that I released them also.

I drove this car that my son gave me for two years and during that time I probably spent ten dollars on it besides the gas and oil, of course. Our financial condition soon became fluid, and Mark wanted me to buy a new car, but I was so attached to my miracle car that I couldn't seem to give it up. One day I was visiting my niece who lived in the hills at the end of Chatsworth, which seemed like the end of nowhere to me. Her car had given out on her completely and wasn't even worth repairing, she said. Here she was way up in the hills with a baby and no means of transportation until her husband came home after working late.

As I was driving back to Hollywood, I knew that I would have to give my precious car to my niece. I told Mark the situation, and he agreed that Jean should have the car. Mark knew that I always loved a Thunderbird, so the next day he purchased a blue one for me. That very evening we drove out and gave Jean my other car. She was delighted. I handed her the pink slip, just as my son did for me. Jean drove that car for about three years and said that every moment with it was a joy. Their financial situation improved too, and her husband purchased another car for her. She sold the "miracle" car to a young teenager who went whistling away, delighted with it.

I am going into detail on this to show how beautiful life can be, if we will only turn with all our hearts and souls to God and His Angels. Absolutely nothing is impossible to us as we *release* our entire lives and every situation over to God!

My definition of the word re-lease is to turn over a new leaf, and take a new lease on life.